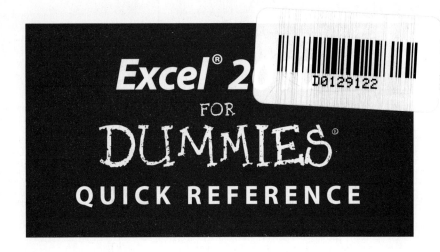

Excel® 2
FOR
DUMMIES®
QUICK REFERENCE

by Colin Banfield and John Walkenbach

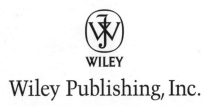

WILEY

Wiley Publishing, Inc.

Excel® 2010 For Dummies® Quick Reference

Published by
Wiley Publishing, Inc.
111 River Street
Hoboken, NJ 07030-5774

www.wiley.com

Copyright © 2010 by Wiley Publishing, Inc., Indianapolis, Indiana

Published by Wiley Publishing, Inc., Indianapolis, Indiana

Published simultaneously in Canada

For general information on our other products and services, please contact our Customer Care Department within the U.S. at 877-762-2974, outside the U.S. at 317-572-3993, or fax 317-572-4002.

For technical support, please visit www.wiley.com/techsupport.

Wiley also publishes its books in a variety of electronic formats. Some content that appears in print may not be available in electronic books.

Library of Congress Control Number: 2010923562

ISBN: 978-0-470-52755-9

Manufactured in the United States of America

10 9 8 7 6 5 4 3 2 1

WILEY

About the Authors

Colin Banfield has worked in the telecommunications field and has been using spreadsheet programs for more than two decades. Colin works with organizations to build business intelligence models, dashboards, and complex adjunct tools using a combination of Excel, Microsoft Access, and other related Microsoft software. In his spare time, Colin writes and reviews books for Wiley and enjoys photography, astronomy, and expanding his musical repertoire. Colin holds a BSc (Honors) in Electrical Engineering from the University of the West Indies and has received extensive training in many advanced technologies. You can reach Colin at www.biexcel.com.

John Walkenbach is a leading authority on spreadsheet software and is principal of JWalk and Associates Inc., a small San Diego–based consulting firm that specializes in spreadsheet application development. He is the author of approximately three dozen spreadsheet books and has written hundreds of articles and reviews for a variety of publications, including *PC World*, *InfoWorld*, *Windows* magazine, and *PC/Computing*. John graduated from the University of Missouri and earned a master's and a PhD from the University of Montana. Visit his Web site at www.j-walk.com.

Dedication

To Dorothy, my most loving and patient better half, and one of the nicest people on the planet. —C. B.

Author's Acknowledgments

Thanks to the folks at Wiley who helped with this book. In particular, my project editor, Susan Pink (Pinkie to me), did her usual wonderful editing and coordinating job and kept me on my toes (not to mention on time). Pinkie has a keen eye for even the smallest details. I'm indebted to Mike Talley, who provided a thorough technical review, spotted important errors, and made some useful suggestions. —C. B.

Publisher's Acknowledgments

We're proud of this book; please send us your comments through our online registration form located at http://dummies.custhelp.com. For other comments, please contact our Customer Care Department within the U.S. at 877-762-2974, outside the U.S. at 317-572-3993, or fax 317-572-4002.

Some of the people who helped bring this book to market include the following:

Acquisitions and Editorial

Project Editor: Susan Pink

Acquisitions Editor: Katie Mohr

Copy Editor: Susan Pink

Technical Editor: Mike Talley

Editorial Manager: Jodi Jensen

Editorial Assistant: Amanda Graham

Sr. Editorial Assistant: Cherie Case

Composition Services

Project Coordinator: Kristie Rees

Layout and Graphics: Christin Swinford, Christine Williams

Proofreaders: Leeann Harney

Indexer: Becky Hornyak

Publishing and Editorial for Technology Dummies

    Richard Swadley, Vice President and Executive Group Publisher

    Andy Cummings, Vice President and Publisher

    Mary Bednarek, Executive Acquisitions Director

    Mary C. Corder, Editorial Director

Publishing for Consumer Dummies

    Diane Graves Steele, Vice President and Publisher

Composition Services

    Debbie Stailey, Director of Composition Services

Table of Contents

Getting to Know Excel 2010

With Microsoft's popular Excel spreadsheet program, you can enter, manipulate, and analyze data in ways that would be impossible, cumbersome, or error prone for you to do manually. This part gives you the basics you need to get up and running quickly in Excel.

In this part . . .

- Familiarizing Yourself with the Excel 2010 Window
- Navigating with the Mouse and Keyboard
- Introducing the Ribbon, Quick Access Toolbar, and Backstage View
- Formatting with Themes and Previewing Your Formatting Live

Excel 2010 Basics

Excel documents are known as *workbooks.* A single workbook can store as many sheets as will fit into memory, and these sheets are stacked like the pages in a notebook. Sheets can be either *worksheets* (a normal spreadsheet-type sheet with rows and columns) or *chart sheets* (a special sheet that holds a single chart).

Most of the time, you perform tasks in worksheets. Each worksheet uses a grid with 1,048,576 rows and 16,384 columns. Excel numbers rows starting with 1 and assigns letters to columns starting with A. After Excel exhausts the letters of the alphabet, column lettering continues with AA, AB, and so on. So column 1 is A, column 26 is Z, column 27 is AA, column 52 is AZ, column 53 is BA, and so on. Rows are numbered from 1 to 1,048,576, and columns are labeled from A to XFD.

The intersection of a row and a column is called a *cell.* A quick calculation using Excel tells us that this works out to 17,179,869,184 cells — more than enough for just about any use. Cells have *addresses,* which are based on their row and column. The upper-left cell in a worksheet is called A1, and the cell down at the bottom right is called XFD1048576. Cell K9 (also known as the dog cell) is the intersection of the eleventh column and the ninth row.

You might be wondering about the amount of system memory (known as random access memory, or RAM) you need to accommodate all those rows and columns. The memory you need depends on the amount of data you store in the workbook and the number of open workbooks. In Excel 2010, the memory available is limited by the maximum amount of memory that your version of Windows (XP, Vista, or Windows 7) can use.

Formulas

A cell in Excel can hold a number, some text, a formula, or nothing at all. You already know what numbers and text are, but you may be a bit fuzzy on the concept of a formula. A *formula* tells Excel to perform a calculation using information stored in other cells. For example, you can insert a formula that tells Excel to add the values in the first 10 cells in column A and to display the result in the cell that contains the formula.

Formulas can use normal arithmetic operators such as + (plus), – (minus), * (multiply), and / (divide). They can also use special built-in functions that let you do powerful things without much effort on your part. For example, Excel has functions that add a range of values, calculate square roots, compute loan payments, and even tell you the time of day. Excel has more than 300 built-in functions, which are categorized by type — Math, Financial, Statistical and so on. Part 5 covers the basics of using functions in Excel.

Active cell and ranges

In Excel, one of the cells in a worksheet is always the active cell. The *active cell* is the one that's selected, and it's displayed with a thicker border than the others. Its contents appear in the *formula bar*. You can select a group, or *range,* of cells by clicking and dragging the mouse pointer over them. You can then issue a command that does something to the active cell or to the range.

The selected range is usually a group of contiguous cells, but it doesn't have to be. To select a noncontiguous group of cells, select the first cell or group of cells, hold down the Ctrl key while you drag the mouse, and select the next cell or group of cells.

Familiarizing Yourself with the Excel 2010 Window

Figure 1-1 shows a typical Excel 2010 window, with the important parts labeled. This terminology rears its ugly head throughout the book, so you should review the figure from time to time.

Moving, resizing, and closing windows

When Excel and workbook windows are in a *restored* state (between a maximized and minimized state, that is) you can use the resize handles to adjust the window size to your liking. Move the mouse pointer to the area of the resize handle until the pointer changes to a double-headed arrow, and then drag with the mouse.

You can move the window around the screen by dragging the title bars. **See also** "Navigating with the Mouse and Keyboard," later in this part.

When the active workbook window is maximized, it shares a single Close button with the Excel window. After you click the shared Close button, Excel closes the active workbook.

Exiting Excel

Use any one of the following methods to close the Excel application:

- ✔ Click the Close button on the Excel title bar if one or no workbook is open.
- ✔ Click the File tab and then click the Exit button.
- ✔ Press the Alt key, then press F, and then press X.

Select all button

Control button

Control button — Mouse pointer — Split box

Name box — Formula bar — Help

Quick Access toolbar — Excel title bar — Close

Active cell pointer — Column header — Workbook title bar — Maximize/Restore

Workbook window — Minimize

Figure 1-1

Sheet tabs — Status bar — Tab split — Zoom controls

Row header — New sheet tab — Scroll bar — Split box

Tab scrolling controls — Normal view — Page break preview

Ribbon — Page layout view

Window resize handles

Navigating with the Mouse and Keyboard

The mouse is the primary tool that you use in Excel for executing commands, making selections, and navigating in the worksheet. Following are the mouse conventions that we use in this book:

- **Click:** Click the left mouse button once.

- **Double-click:** Click the left mouse button twice in quick succession.

- **Right-click:** Click the right mouse button once.

- **Drag:** Hold down the left mouse button and move the mouse. Release the mouse button to complete the drag operation.

- **Hover:** Place the mouse pointer over an element without clicking a mouse button.

- **Select:** Place the mouse pointer over an element and click the left mouse button.

Mousing around

Every mouse action is associated with some element in the Excel window. An *element* can be a slider, button, cell, chart object, and so on. You select or hover over the element using the mouse pointer.

Navigating through a worksheet with a mouse works just as you'd expect. Click a cell, and it becomes the active cell. If the cell that you want to activate isn't visible in the workbook window, you can use the scroll bars to scroll the window in any direction, as follows:

- To scroll one cell, click one of the arrows on the scroll bar.

- To scroll by a complete screen, click either side of the scroll bar's slider.

- To scroll faster, drag the slider.

- To scroll a long distance vertically, press and hold the Shift key while dragging the slider button.

Note that only the active workbook window displays scroll bars. If you activate a different window, its scroll bars appear.

After you right-click a cell, a range of cells, or another object in the worksheet area, Excel displays a *contextual* menu, so-called because the menu includes commands specific to working with the cell, range, or object.

For your convenience, Excel adds a minitoolbar above the contextual menu with useful commands drawn from the Ribbon, as shown in Figure 1-2. ***See also*** "Introducing the Ribbon," later in this part.

Figure 1-2

Using the keyboard

Most users will be comfortable using the mouse to do all their work in Excel. For users who prefer to use the keyboard exclusively when working in Windows applications or for users who prefer to split the use of the mouse and keyboard among various tasks, Excel provides the following solutions:

- ✔ Keyboard shortcuts
- ✔ Keyboard navigation
- ✔ KeyTips

The first two functions are described next. For more on the last function, KeyTips, *see* "Tipping off your keyboard," later in this part.

You can access commands in Excel using *keyboard shortcuts,* which are individual keystrokes or a combination of keys pressed simultaneously. To access the Print command using a shortcut, for example, you hold down the Ctrl key and press the P key, represented in this book as Ctrl+P. The following table lists some common keyboard shortcuts in Excel.

Shortcut	*Action*
Ctrl+A	Select all
Ctrl+B	Apply or remove bold formatting
Ctrl+C	Copy selection
Ctrl+F	Find
Ctrl+G or F5	Go to

Shortcut	*Action*
Ctrl+H	Replace
Ctrl+I	Apply or remove italic formatting
Ctrl+O or Ctrl+F12	Open a document
Ctrl+P	Print
Ctrl+S or Shift+F12	Save
Ctrl+U	Apply or remove underlining
Ctrl+V	Paste
Ctrl+W or Ctrl+F4	Close the active workbook
Crtl+X	Cut
Ctrl+Y or F4	Repeat the last action
Ctrl+Z	Undo the last action
F1	Display the help viewer
Ctrl+F1	Hide or display the Ribbon commands
F2	Enable editing within the active cell

With more than 17 billion cells in a worksheet, you need ways to move to specific cells. Fortunately, Excel provides you with many techniques to move around a worksheet. As always, you can use either your mouse or the keyboard on your navigational journeys. The following table lists the keystrokes that enable you to move through a worksheet.

Keys	*Action*
Up arrow	Moves the active cell one row up
Down arrow	Moves the active cell one row down
Left arrow	Moves the active cell one column to the left
Right arrow	Moves the active cell one column to the right
PgUp	Moves the active cell one screen up
PgDn	Moves the active cell one screen down
Alt+PgDn	Moves the active cell one screen right
Alt+PgUp	Moves the active cell one screen left
Home	Moves the active cell to the first column of the row that the active cell is currently in
Ctrl+Home	Moves the active cell to the beginning of worksheet (A1)
F5	Displays the Go To dialog box

cont.

Keys	Action
Ctrl+Backspace	Scrolls the screen to display the active cell
Up arrow*	Scrolls the screen one row up (active cell doesn't change)
Down arrow*	Scrolls the screen one row down (active cell doesn't change)
Left arrow*	Scrolls the screen one column left (active cell doesn't change)
Right arrow*	Scrolls the screen one column right (active cell doesn't change)

* With Scroll Lock on

Introducing the Ribbon

Excel comes with a user interface called the *Ribbon,* which consists of a series of horizontal tabs, each containing a variety of commands grouped according to function (see Figure 1-3). Most features in Excel 2010 are available through the commands on the Ribbon tabs.

Home tab

Contextual tab header

Figure 1-3

Split button

Dialog launcher

Contextual tabs

Dissecting the parts of the Ribbon

The commands on the Ribbon are accessed through a variety of *controls.* Here's a list of the various types of controls and other parts that make up the Ribbon:

 ✔ **Button:** This is the most common type of control. Most buttons on the Ribbon (except the formatting ones) have descriptive text associated with them, so you don't need to be a Mensa expert to figure out what a button represents. The most frequently used commands on each Ribbon tab have larger buttons.

 Most buttons execute commands directly when you click them. However, some buttons have an embedded downward-pointing arrow, and others have an attached downward-pointing arrow. Clicking a button with an embedded arrow displays a menu or gallery. For a button with an attached arrow (known as a *split button*), the icon or text part of the button represents the most common command for the button. Clicking the arrow part displays a menu or gallery with additional commands or formatting choices. The two types of buttons with arrows look similar, but if you hover the mouse pointer over a button with an attached arrow, you see a clear delineation between the icon or text (command) part and the arrow (menu) part (refer to Figure 1-3).

✔ **Check box:** This is a square box that you click to turn an option on or off.

✔ **Command group:** Each Ribbon tab contains groups of related commands. For example, you find commands related to text fonts in the Font group of the Home tab.

✔ **Dialog launcher:** A *dialog launcher* is a command that launches a dialog box (a pop-up window) from a command group, menu, or gallery. The dialog launcher in a command group is a little button in the bottom right of the group frame. In addition, some menus and galleries contain options that launch dialog boxes. After you click a dialog launcher, a dialog box appears that presents additional choices. (However, the Ribbon displays the commands you are likely to use frequently, thus minimizing the need to launch dialog boxes.)

✔ **Drop-down list:** This list contains things you can choose from. Click the control's downward-pointing arrow to display the list.

✔ **Gallery:** A *gallery* is a control that presents you with a set of graphic choices, such as a particular formatting style (patterns, colors, and effects) or a predefined layout. An example of a predefined layout is a chart choice with specific elements preselected for inclusion in the chart. Galleries enable Excel to be more results oriented; that is, they present the likely result you are looking for first and then expose advanced choices through a dialog box or Ribbon command.

Three types of galleries are available:

• **Drop-down gallery:** This is displayed after you click certain buttons with downward-pointing arrows. This type of gallery presents a single column of choices and includes both graphic and text elements.

• **Drop-down grid:** This is displayed after you click certain buttons with downward-pointing arrows. This type of gallery presents a two-dimensional grid of choices and does not include text.

• **In-Ribbon gallery:** This is like the drop-down grid, but this gallery exposes a single row of choices directly within a Ribbon control group. You can click up and down scroll arrows to reveal additional rows, or you can click a drop-down arrow to display the full set of choices in a two-dimensional grid.

✔ **Menu, rich:** Rich menus have illustrative graphics, the command name, and in some cases a short description of what the command does.

Remember: Don't confuse rich menus with drop-down galleries, although they look similar. Menus contain related *commands*. Galleries allow you to choose from among a set of formats or layouts.

✔ **Menu, standard:** Most users are already familiar with this form of menu — a drop-down list of choices with command names (such as Copy or Insert Cells). Some command names have small associated icons. If you click a command name that ends with an ellipsis (...), Excel displays a dialog box that presents further choices.

✔ **Spinner:** A spinner is a control with two arrows (one pointing up, the other pointing down) used with an input box to specify a number (height or width, for example.) Clicking an arrow increases or decreases the number in the input box. You can also enter a number in the box directly. The spinner control allows you to use only valid numbers.

✔ **Tab, contextual:** Contextual tabs give the Ribbon the power to expose most Excel features. One or more contextual tabs appear after you insert or select an object, such as a chart, shape, table, or picture. For example, after you insert a chart, three contextual tabs related to chart functionality appear on the Ribbon and a header labeled Chart Tools appears on the Excel title bar above the contextual tabs. Contextual tabs contain all the commands you need for working with the particular object. After you deselect an object, the contextual tabs (and the header) disappear.

The general rules that govern the display of contextual tabs follow:

- After you select an object (such as a chart, shape, or table), one or more contextual tabs for the object appear on the Ribbon. You must select a tab to display the associated commands.

- After you insert an object, Excel displays the commands for the first tab of the contextual tab set for that object.

- After you double-click an object, Excel displays the commands for the first tab of the contextual tab set for that object. Note that not all objects have this double-click capability.

- After you select, deselect, and then reselect the object without using any other commands in-between, Excel displays the commands for the first tab of the contextual tab set for that object.

✔ **Tab, custom:** In addition to the built-in standard and contextual Ribbon tabs that Excel includes, you can create custom Ribbon tabs.

✔ **Tab, standard:** The Ribbon comes with a set of standard tabs, each organized according to the functions of the commands that it contains. For example, the Insert tab contains command groups to insert shapes, charts, tables, pictures, and so on. An exception is the Home tab, which is so-named because this is where you do most of your work in Excel.

If your mouse has a scroll wheel, you can navigate quickly among the Ribbon tabs by hovering the mouse pointer over the Ribbon area and scrolling the wheel back and forth.

✔ **Text box:** A box in which you enter a number or text. In general, the Ribbon associates a text box with another control, such as a spinner or a drop-down box.

Sizing up the Ribbon

The layout of the Ribbon controls is not static. Depending on your screen resolution, or the Excel window size, or both, the Ribbon provides one of four layout options for command groups. If sufficient space is available, the Ribbon presents a layout that labels commands, displays more commands individually, and eliminates extra mouse clicks. As you resize the Ribbon downwards (by reducing the screen resolution or shrinking the size of the Excel window), the Ribbon rearranges the layout of some of the command groups by first resizing command buttons (larger buttons become smaller), then removing labels from commands, and finally reducing the groups to single large buttons (see Figure 1-4). To access the commands in a command group that the Ribbon resizes to a single button, you must first click the button to display a menu and then select the command.

Figure 1-4

It is important to note that at each stage of downward resizing, no command groups or commands disappear entirely from the Ribbon. The multiple layout options for the command groups ensure that nothing is lost as space becomes more limited. If you reduce the size of the Excel window sufficiently, however, the Ribbon disappears altogether.

Tipping off your keyboard

Excel provides KeyTips, which allow you to access every command on the Ribbon using the keyboard, without having to memorize keystroke combinations! So, what are KeyTips? *KeyTips* are little alphanumerical indicators containing a single letter, a single number, a combination of two letters, or a combination of a letter and a number, indicating what to type to activate the command under them, as shown in Figure 1-5.

Figure 1-5

Follow these steps to access a command on a Ribbon tab using a KeyTip:

1. Press the Alt key. The KeyTips appear over the Ribbon tabs. (Ignore the KeyTips that appear in the other areas of the user interface for this exercise.)

2. Press the key that represents the KeyTip for the Ribbon tab that you want to access. For example, press N to select the Insert tab. Note that you *do not* have to hold down the Alt key. If you need to select a different tab after you select the KeyTip for a tab, press the Esc key.

3. Press the key or key combination that represents the KeyTip for the command you want to use.

If the command you select is a drop-down gallery or drop-down grid, you can use an arrow key or the Tab key to highlight your choice and then press the Enter key to select your choice.

Remember: KeyTips are associated with in-Ribbon galleries, so you have to press the key that represents the KeyTip for the gallery before you can choose an option in the gallery.

Hiding the Ribbon commands

If you find that the Ribbon commands take up too much room in the Excel window, you can hide them using any of the following methods:

✔ Click the Ribbon's Minimize button in the Excel title bar (to the left of the help button)

✔ Press Ctrl+F1

✔ Double-click any Ribbon tab

✔ Right-click in the Ribbon area and choose Minimize the Ribbon from the contextual menu

After you hide the commands, only the Ribbon tabs are displayed. If you click a tab after you hide the Ribbon commands, Excel displays the tab commands temporarily. The commands are hidden again after you select a command in the tab or click away from the Ribbon area. Similarly, you can use KeyTips to select a command when the command display is hidden.

To redisplay the commands permanently after you hide them, use the same methods described for hiding the commands.

Remember: Excel maintains the hidden condition of the Ribbon commands if you exit and subsequently relaunch Excel.

Introducing the Quick Access Toolbar (QAT)

The Quick Access toolbar (or QAT) is an area of the user interface that provides quick access to commands. The QAT is designed to reduce the amount of navigation you have to do in the Ribbon to access the features that you use frequently. The QAT is located at the top left of the Excel title bar, above the Ribbon tabs (see Figure 1-6).

Figure 1-6

The QAT contains three default commands (Save, Undo, and Redo); you can add additional commands.

Follow these steps to add a command to the QAT:

1. Select the Ribbon tab that houses the command you want to add.

2. Right-click the command and choose Add to Quick Access Toolbar in the menu that appears.

To quickly add some commonly used commands to the QAT, click the arrow to the right of the toolbar and choose a command from the menu.

You can add an entire Ribbon command group to the QAT. Just right-click an area in the command group name (for example, Font) and choose Add to Quick Access Toolbar.

Follow these steps to remove a command (including the default commands) from the toolbar:

1. Right-click the command you want to remove from the toolbar.

2. Choose Remove from Quick Access Toolbar in the menu that appears.

 If you think you'll be adding a lot of commands to the QAT, it's a good idea to move the toolbar from the title bar to a separate location below the Ribbon. Right-click anywhere on the QAT and choose Place Quick Access Toolbar below the Ribbon in the menu that appears. You can regain screen area for working in the worksheet by hiding the Ribbon controls temporarily.

You can access commands on the Quick Access toolbar using the keyboard. Press the Alt key and then a number key that represents the KeyTip for the command you want to access. **See also** "Tipping off your keyboard," earlier in this part.

Going Backstage

 Excel 2010 introduces a new view for working with documents called the Backstage view. This view is accessed by clicking the File tab on the Ribbon. See Figure 1-7.

The Backstage view consolidates all document management tasks, such as opening, closing, and sharing files; printing; and setting document properties. In previous versions of Excel, many of these tasks were scattered all over the user interface.

On the left side of Backstage view is a *navigation pane* that consists of a mix of *quick command* buttons (such as open, close, and save) and vertically aligned tabs (Info, Recent, New, Print, Send & Save, and Help). The buttons execute commands directly, and the vertical tabs, like traditional horizontal tabs, expose a set of options. If you don't have any workbooks currently open, some of the buttons and tabs will be disabled.

A distinguishing feature of Backstage view is that while you work in this view, no part of the worksheet is visible. Also, Excel minimizes the Ribbon (assuming that you haven't previously minimized the Ribbon yourself). To return to the worksheet display view, click any Ribbon tab or press Esc.

Figure 1-7

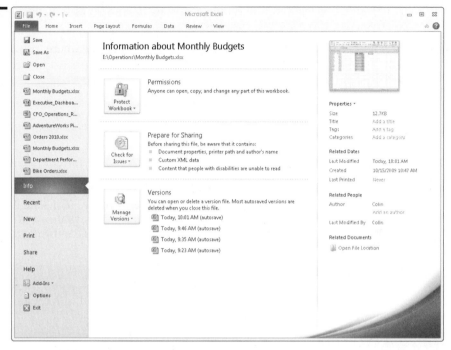

The Backstage navigation pane includes an Options button, which gives you access to various Excel options. We encourage you to visit the options from time to time because you may find useful application, workbook, or worksheet options that you want to turn on or off. An option in the Advanced tab of the Excel Options dialog box, for example, allows you to increase the number of documents displayed in the Recent Workbooks list to a maximum of 50. You'll find a list of recent workbooks in the Backstage Recent tab.

Previewing Your Formatting Live

When you hover over a formatting option with the mouse pointer, Excel lets you see the effect that the formatting option will have on your selection *before* you commit to applying the option. This feature is called *Live Preview*. Your selection for Live Preview might be a cell, a range of cells, a chart, a table, a shape, and more.

Suppose that you want to change the font of some text in a cell. On the Ribbon, a drop-down box called the font picker presents a list of available fonts. As you hover over each choice in the font picker, your cell updates to show you what the text would look like if you chose that font. Live Preview avoids the normal tedium of committing to an option, then undoing the option because the result is not what you wanted, and then committing to another option, only to realize that you don't like the new result either, and so on.

You find Live Preview options throughout Excel in places where formatting alternatives are available — most notably in galleries.

Remember: Live Preview formatting is not universal in Excel. Some elements provide formatting alternatives but do not have Live Preview support.

Formatting with Themes

In Excel, you can use a formatting concept known as a theme. A *theme* consists of a combination of fonts, colors, and effects that provide a consistent look among your workbook's elements, including cells, charts, tables, and PivotTables. You apply the theme's fonts, colors, and effects through individual options or the style galleries of the various elements.

Excel applies a default theme to all new workbooks along with a theme gallery so that you can change the default theme. After you select a new theme, all galleries and all the elements in your workbook formatted with theme styles change to match the new theme.

Following is a description of the three parts of a theme:

  ✔ **Theme font:** A theme uses two complementary fonts — a header font and a body font. All elements using themed styles use the same font or fonts. Click the arrow on the drop-down box (the font picker) on the Ribbon's Home tab to see the fonts used in the theme currently applied to the workbook.

  ✔ **Theme color:** A theme uses a matched set of twelve colors. Click the arrow on the Fill Color or Font Color tool in the Font group of the Home tab to see ten of the colors used in the theme currently applied to the workbook (see Figure 1-8).

Figure 1-8

The following are characteristics of theme colors:

- The top row in a color picker displays the base theme colors, and the next five rows display various tints and shades of the base colors. Below the theme colors are standard colors that do not change if the theme is changed. If you want to apply specific formatting that doesn't change after you change the theme, use a standard color.

- The first four columns of colors on the picker (from the left) are intended for text and background use. These colors are designed so that light text always shows well on a dark background, and vice versa.

- The next six columns of colors are used for accents. Most of the theme-style galleries in Excel make extensive use of accent colors.

The two colors that are not displayed on the color pickers are used for hyperlinks (not discussed in this book).

- ✔ **Theme effect:** Theme effects apply to graphic elements such as charts and shapes and include three levels of styles for outlines, fills, and special effects. Special effects include shadow, glow, bevel, and reflection.

You can change the theme in a workbook by clicking the Themes button on the Ribbon's Page Layout tab and selecting a new theme from the gallery that appears.

Remember: The Microsoft Office applications — Excel 2010, Word 2010, PowerPoint 2010, and Access 2010 — share the same themes. If you create reports that combine elements from each application, your reports will have a consistent look if you use a common theme.

Soliciting Help

With so many features and options available in Excel, it isn't unusual to get stuck once in a while. Fortunately, Excel provides the following methods for getting help easily:

- ✔ **SuperTips:** Standard ScreenTips (also called ToolTips), which have been available in Excel (and many other Windows applications) for some time, provide textual context to commands. After hovering your mouse pointer over a command having a standard ScreenTip, Excel displays the action of the command using either a single word (such as *Paste*) or a brief phrase (such as *Increase Font Size*). A standard ScreenTip helps to decipher the meaning of a command button, for example, when the button has no associated text and the command meaning is unclear from the button icon.

SuperTips take the concept a step further by adding a short description explaining the purpose of the command. Some SuperTips include an explanatory graphic when a text description is insufficient to explain the meaning of the command. SuperTips are available for all commands on the Ribbon. In many cases, the SuperTip explanation provides enough information so you don't have to seek additional help.

✔ **Contextual help:** If the SuperTip doesn't offer enough for you to understand the use of a specific command, you can get more detailed help. After you hover the mouse pointer over the command, the SuperTip that pops up lets you know whether additional help for the command is available by indicating that you can press F1 for more help.

If you are in a dialog box and need help for the dialog box options, click the help button on the dialog box's title bar (the question mark) to get contextual help.

✔ **General help:** Click the help button (the question mark) on the right side of the Excel title bar or press F1 when you are not in a specific context (for example, the mouse pointer is not hovering over a command on the Ribbon) to display a list of general help topics.

✔ **Backstage help:** You can access additional help topics in Backstage view. Click the File tab on the Ribbon and then click the Help tab. The Help tab consolidates the following help components:

- **Support:** This option provides various ways to get Excel help and troubleshoot issues.

- **Tools for Working with Office:** In this section, you can access general Excel options or check online for product updates.

- **Product Licensing Status:** This component displays the Office 2010 products you are licensed to use on your computer, the applications included in each installed product suite, and the activation status of the products.

- **About Microsoft Excel:** This component displays information that assists Microsoft Customer Service and Support in diagnosing any issues you are having with Excel. When you use contextual help or general help, Excel displays the help viewer, shown in Figure 1-9. The viewer sports Internet browser-style controls. In fact, it was built using the same technology that Microsoft uses in its Internet Explorer browser application. The viewer is not a full-fledged browser because you can view only Excel help content.

Figure 1-9

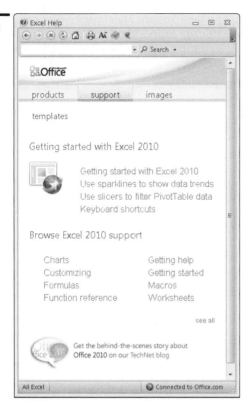

Although most of the options in the help viewer are self-explanatory, the following options require further discussion:

- ✔ **Search box:** You can enter specific search text in this box. The viewer stores a list of your text searches for the current help session. Click the drop-down arrow on the side of the box to view and select an item from the list if you want to review a previous search result.

- ✔ **Search split button:** Click the text part of the Search split button (or press Enter) to initiate a search after you enter the search text in the search box. Click the arrow part of the Search split button to define the search scope. By default, if your computer is connected to the Internet, Excel will display help content from an online source. If possible, you should use this source as your first choice because Microsoft updates the contents of online help regularly.

If you're offline when you initiate a search, Excel uses help content internal to your system. Whether online or offline, you can narrow your search scope further by selecting an appropriate option from the Search button menu.

✔ **Status bar:** The left side of the status bar (located at the bottom of the help viewer) displays the current search scope. On the right side of the status bar is a connection status button that displays the current connection status (online or offline). You can click this button to switch quickly between viewing online and offline help content.

✔ **Pin button:** By default, Excel keeps the help viewer window on top when you're working in an application. Use the Pin button to control this behavior. If you "unpin" the viewer by clicking the button, Excel hides the window automatically if you click anywhere inside the Excel window.

If you want to resize the help viewer window, move the mouse pointer to any edge of the window until the pointer changes to a double-headed arrow, and then drag the mouse.

Managing Workbooks

Working with documents is critical to using any software. Microsoft Excel documents are known as *workbooks*. This part covers the procedures that you need to know to manage workbook documents efficiently.

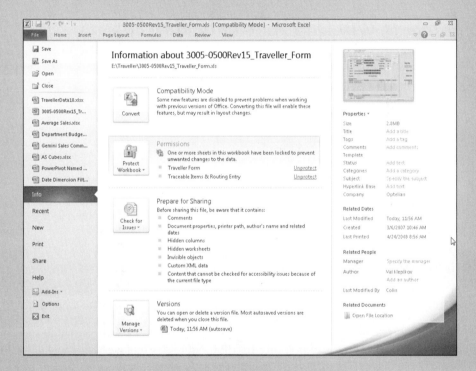

In this part . . .

- ✔ **Comparing Two Workbooks Side by Side**
- ✔ **Creating Multiple Windows (Views) for a Workbook**
- ✔ **Opening and Saving Workbooks**
- ✔ **Protecting and Unprotecting a Workbook**
- ✔ **Sharing Workbooks**
- ✔ **Working with Workbook Templates**

Activating a Workbook

A workbook is *active* when its window is maximized in the Excel window or after you select any part of the workbook when its window is not maximized. *See also* "Familiarizing Yourself with the Excel 2010 Window," in Part 1 and "Switching among Open Workbooks," later in this part.

Arranging Windows Automatically

If you want all your open workbook windows visible on-screen, you can move and resize them manually — or you can have Excel do it automatically. Follow these steps to make all open workbooks visible on the Excel screen:

1. Click the View tab on the Ribbon.

2. Click the Arrange All button. Excel displays the Arrange Windows dialog box.

3. Choose from the Tiled, Horizontal, Vertical, or Cascade options.

4. Click OK.

See also "Comparing Two Workbooks Side by Side," later in this part.

Changing the Default File Location

When you're opening a document in Excel, by default the Open dialog box points to the My Documents folder (Windows XP) or the Documents folder (Windows Vista and Windows 7) as the starting location to open documents. If you keep frequently used documents in a different folder, you may want the Open dialog box to point to this different folder to save some navigation steps. To change the default folder, follow these steps:

1. Click the File tab on the Ribbon, and then click the Options button. The Excel Options dialog box appears. The options are divided into vertically aligned tabs on the left side of the dialog box.

2. Click the Save tab.

3. In the Default File Location text box, enter the path of the new default starting location to open documents. For example, if your new default document location is in a subfolder named Excel, which itself is in the My Documents or Documents folder, add \Excel to the default path. The new location in the text box should read C:\Users*Username*\Documents\Excel, where *Username* is the name of the user indicated in the text box.

4. Click OK.

Closing a Workbook

If you're no longer working with a workbook, you may want to close the workbook so that you can work on other documents without distraction. Closing unneeded workbooks also frees memory and minimizes potential screen clutter.

To close the unneeded workbook or workbooks, follow these steps:

1. If multiple workbooks are open, ensure that the workbook you want to close is active as follows: Click the View tab on the Ribbon, click the Switch Windows button, and select the workbook from the list of names in the menu.

2. Use any of the following methods to close the workbook:

   - Click the File tab on the Ribbon and then choose Close.

   - Click the Close button on the right side of the Excel title bar (or the right side of the workbook's title bar if the workbook is not maximized).

   - Double-click the Control button on the far left of the workbook's title bar if the workbook is not maximized.

   - Press Ctrl+F4.

   - Press Ctrl+W.

If you've made any changes to your workbook since the last time you saved it, Excel asks whether you want to save the changes before closing the workbook.

Comparing Two Workbooks Side by Side

Sometimes you have two versions of a workbook, and you want to compare the differences in the data visually. Excel provides a convenient feature that allows you to compare two documents side by side. To use this feature, follow these steps:

1. Open the workbooks you want to compare.

2. Click the View tab on the Ribbon and then click the View Side by Side button. Excel arranges the windows of the two workbooks horizontally. If you have more than two workbooks open, Excel displays a dialog box from which you select the name of the workbook you want to compare with the active workbook.

3. Click a worksheet tab in each workbook to display the worksheet data you want to compare.

4. In the View tab, click the Synchronous Scrolling button to toggle synchronized scrolling on and off. After you enable synchronized scrolling, the rows and columns in the two worksheets being compared scroll simultaneously.

5. You can click the Reset Window Position button on the View tab to ensure that the two workbook windows are sized equally and aligned horizontally. You need to use the button only if you adjust either or both window sizes during the current session.

Creating a New (Empty) Workbook

After you start Excel, it automatically creates a new (empty) workbook that it calls Book1. If you're starting a new project from scratch, you can use this blank workbook.

You can create another blank workbook in the following ways:

> ✔ Press Ctrl+N.

> ✔ Click the File tab on the Ribbon, click the New tab in the Backstage navigation pane, and either double-click Blank Workbook in the Available Templates section or select Blank Workbook and click the Create button on the right side of window.

You can add a button to the Quick Access toolbar (QAT) that allows you to create a blank workbook with a single mouse click. Click the arrow to the right of the QAT and choose New from the menu. Excel adds the New button to the toolbar. *See also* "Working with the Quick Access Toolbar (QAT)," in Part 1.

Creating Multiple Windows (Views) for a Workbook

Sometimes, you want to view two parts of the *same* worksheet at once. Or you want to see more than one sheet in the same workbook simultaneously. You can accomplish either action by displaying your workbook in one or more additional windows.

To create a new view of the active workbook, click the View tab on the Ribbon and then click the New Window button. Excel displays a new window for the active workbook. To help you keep track of the windows, Excel appends a colon and a number to the workbook name in each window, as shown in Figure 2-1.

Figure 2-1

See also "Arranging Windows Automatically" and "Comparing Two Documents Side by Side," both earlier in this part.

Remember: A single workbook can have as many views (that is, separate windows) as you want.

Displaying multiple windows for a workbook also makes copying information from one worksheet to another easier. You can use Excel's drag-and-drop procedures to copy a cell, a range, or a chart. **See also** "Copying Cells and Ranges," in Part 4, and "Resizing, Moving, Copying, and Deleting an Embedded Chart," in Part 10.

Opening Non-native Files

In addition to files in its native format, Excel can open files in non-native Excel 2010 formats, including older Excel and text files. Excel can open files that weren't saved in its native format by using filters to open the foreign file as a workbook document.

To open a file in a non-Excel 2010 format, follow these steps:

1. Click the File tab on the Ribbon and then choose Open. Excel displays the Open dialog box.

2. Windows XP: In the Files of Type drop-down list, select the file type.

   Windows Vista and Windows 7: Click the button located above the Open and Cancel buttons and choose a file type from the menu. By default, the button text reads All Excel Files (*.xl*;*.xlsx;*.xlsm), but the text changes if you select a different file type.

3. Windows XP: In the Look In drop-down list, navigate to the folder that contains the file.

Windows Vista and Windows 7: In the Folders window on the left side of the dialog box, navigate to the folder that contains the document.

4. Select the file and click Open, or double-click the filename.

See also "Opening a Workbook," immediately following this section.

Opening a Workbook

If you open a workbook in Excel, the entire document loads into memory, and any changes that you make occur only in the copy that's in memory. During the file open process, the workbook undergoes security checks. If Excel detects a potential security issue, it will open the workbook in one of two ways:

✔ After opening the workbook, a security warning message is displayed in the Message bar. Security warnings appear if Excel detects *active* content in the workbook. The most common active content you're likely to encounter are macros, ActiveX components (a type of software code), and external data connections.

✔ Excel opens the workbook in protected mode. In *protected mode,* you can view but not edit the contents of the workbook (it's read-only and all Ribbon controls are disabled). Also, Excel places the workbook in an isolated environment so that any malicious code present cannot get into your system and cause harm. In general, Excel opens the workbook in protected mode if it detects any the following conditions:

- The workbook was downloaded from the Internet. Windows places a marker on a file you download from the Internet, identifying its source.

- The workbook was opened from Outlook 2010.

- The workbook was opened from an unsafe location, such as your Temporary Internet Files folder.

- The workbook was blocked by Excel's File Block policies.

- The workbook fails file validation checks. Excel validates binary files (Excel files with an .xls or .xlt extension) against a well-known structure (called a *schema*). You can change Excel's default handling of files with security issues by modifying settings in the Trust Center. *See* "Modifying security settings in the Trust Center," later in this section.

Opening a workbook using the Open dialog box

To open a workbook, follow these steps:

1. Click the File tab on the Ribbon and then choose Open to display the Open dialog box. Alternatively, press Ctrl+O or Ctrl+F12 to display the Open dialog box.

2. Windows XP: In the Look In drop-down list, navigate to the folder that contains the document.

   Windows Vista and Windows 7: In the Folders window on the left side of the dialog box, navigate to the folder that contains the document (see Figure 2-2).

3. Select the workbook in the selected folder and click Open, or double-click the filename.

TIP

You can select more than one document in the Open dialog box. Hold down Ctrl while you click each document. After you select all the documents you want, click Open.

Figure 2-2

4. If the Message bar appears after the workbook opens, indicating that the workbook has security issues, do the following:

   • If the workbook opens in protected mode, click Enable Editing or click the Protected mode message to go to the Info tab in Backstage view. In Backstage view, you can enable editing or get details about the workbook.

For most messages, the Message bar appears with an amber color. However, the bar appears in red after opening a file that fails validation. The color indicates an elevated security risk and the possibility that the file contains a malicious threat. You should therefore be sure about where the file originated before you enable editing.

- If the security warning is due to active content in the workbook, click Enable Content on the Message bar or click the security warning message. If you click Enable Content, Excel enables the content and removes the warning message. If you instead click the security message, Excel takes you Backstage on the Info tab, where you can examine the type of active content in the workbook and enable each type individually (or not at all).

Remember: If your workbook opens in protected mode *and* has active content, Excel displays the active content security warning after you enable editing.

Remember: After you enable editing or all content for a workbook, Excel 2010 will not display any security warning the next time you open the workbook.

Opening recently used workbooks

You can open a workbook you have worked on recently without navigating through the Open dialog box. In the navigation pane in Backstage view, click the Recent tab. On the Recent tab, Excel displays a list of recently used documents. If the document that you want to open appears in this list, you can open it by double-clicking its name.

By default, Excel places the last 20 documents you used in the recently used list. You can adjust this number in the Excel Options dialog box. Click Options in the Backstage navigation pane. In the Excel Options dialog box that appears, click the Advanced tab and scroll down to the Display section. In the Show This Number of Recent Documents spinner control, enter a number. The maximum number of documents you can have in the list is 50.

After you open more documents than are set to appear in the list, Excel removes documents from the list, beginning with the last document. If you want to keep a document permanently in the list, click the pushpin at the end of the document's name. Click the pushpin again to unpin the document from the list. Right-click any document name to access additional options.

You can place the top x (where x is a number) recently used documents directly in the Backstage navigation pane so you can access these documents quickly. To enable this feature, click the Recent tab in the Backstage navigation pane. At the very bottom of the recently used list area, select the box labeled Quickly Access This Number of Recent Workbooks. Enter the number of workbooks you want to appear on the navigation pane using the spinner control.

Modifying security settings in the Trust Center

Excel allows you to change its default handling of workbooks that have potential security issues. You make these changes in the Trust Center. You can access the Trust Center as follows:

✔ If the workbook opens in protected mode, click the message text that appears in the Message bar to go Backstage. In Backstage view, click the Protected Mode Settings link. Excel displays the Trust Center dialog box with the Protected View tab selected. You can enable and disable Protected mode settings in this tab.

✔ To access all Trust Center settings, click the File tab on the Ribbon and then click Options in the Backstage navigation pane. In the Excel Options dialog box, click the Trust Center tab and then click Trust Center Settings. Excel displays the Trust Center dialog box. Click the various tabs to review and alter settings as required.

Protecting and Unprotecting a Workbook

Excel provides several levels of protection for your work. Here are some ways you can protect your workbooks. You can protect

✔ A workbook from being opened by unauthorized personnel

✔ A workbook from being saved with the same filename

✔ A workbook's structure (control the manipulation of worksheets in a workbook)

✔ A workbook's windows (control the sizing and positioning of a workbook's windows and any workbook views you create)

You should write down any passwords you use and store them in a safe location. If you forget or lose your passwords, you won't be able to undo the areas you protected by any normal means.

Safeguarding your workbook from unauthorized users

Follow these steps to restrict unauthorized personnel from opening or modifying a workbook:

1. Open a workbook or select an already opened workbook you want to protect.

2. Click the File tab on the Ribbon and then click the Info tab.

3. Click Protect Workbook and then choose Encrypt with Password from the menu. Excel displays the Encrypt Document dialog box.

4. Enter a password. For a strong password that's difficult for third-party tools to decrypt, use a minimum of eight characters consisting of uppercase and lowercase letters, numbers, and special characters (for example #, @, and !). However, don't make the password so cryptic that it's impossible to remember.

5. Click OK. Excel asks you to reenter the password for confirmation.

6. Reenter the password you entered in Step 4 and then click OK. In the Permissions section of the Info tab, Excel updates information about the protection status of the workbook.

To remove passwords from the workbook, follow the preceding steps, except delete the password in Step 4.

If you are using a workbook saved in an earlier version of Excel, Excel 2010 displays a message offering to convert the workbook to the Office XML file format (the native file format) before you save the workbook with passwords. Excel offers this choice because the newer file format uses much stronger encryption than the older file format. You should choose to accept the suggestion only if you will not be sharing the workbook with users who use an Excel version earlier than Excel 2007. **See also** "Saving Files," later in this part.

Protecting and unprotecting a workbook structure or window

To protect a workbook structure or window properties from accidental or intentional alteration, follow these steps:

1. Click the Review tab on the Ribbon, click the Protect Workbook button, and then choose Protect Structure and Windows from the menu. Excel displays the Protect Workbook dialog box.

2. Select the appropriate check box(es), as follows:

   - *Structure* prevents any of the following changes to a workbook sheet: adding, deleting, moving, renaming, hiding, or unhiding.

   - *Windows* protects the workbook window from being moved or resized.

3. If you need a high level of protection, supply a password in the Password text box and then click OK. When Excel requests that you reenter the password for confirmation, do so.

4. Click OK.

To unprotect a workbook structure or window, click the Review tab on the Ribbon, click the Protect Workbook button, and then choose Protect Structure and Windows from the menu. If you did not supply a password when the workbook was protected, Excel unprotects the workbook automatically. Otherwise, Excel prompts you to enter a password.

In Excel 2010, you can also protect the workbook structure or window from the Backstage view. Follow Steps 1 to 3 in the procedure outlined for "Safeguarding your workbook from unauthorized users," but in Step 3, choose Protect Workbook Structure from the menu.

Recovering an Unsaved File

Sometimes while you're working in a workbook, Excel crashes or the power fails. To handle these situations, Excel provides the *AutoRecover* feature. After you restart Excel following a program crash or power failure, Excel displays the Document Recovery pane to the left of the worksheet area. The Document Recovery pane lists all worksheets that were open at the time of the crash or outage.

The Document Recovery pane lists both the original version and the autosaved version of each file. The original version is the version you last saved. The autosaved version is the version last saved by AutoRecover. By default, AutoRecover saves a file in ten-minute intervals, if you make changes to the file.

The files listed in the Document Recovery pane include descriptions of the file status (original or autosaved). If you need to see more of the description, move the mouse pointer to the right side of the pane until the pointer changes to a double-headed arrow, and then drag to the right.

Click a file in the pane to open it. If you open the autosaved version and want it to replace the last version you saved, click the Save button in the Quick Access toolbar (QAT). To select a different option for the file (for example, to delete the file or save the file under a different name), hover the mouse pointer over the filename in the pane. When a drop-down arrow appears at the end of the filename, click the arrow and choose an option.

You can change the default autosave interval and modify other AutoRecover settings. Click the File tab on the Ribbon and then click Options in the Backstage navigation pane. In the Excel Options dialog box that appears, click the Save tab. On the Save tab, make the modifications you want.

Excel 2010 saves a separate version of the workbook at each autosave interval. If for any reason you need to recover an older version of your working file, click the File tab on the Ribbon and then click the Info tab. To the right of the Manage Versions button, select the saved version you want to open.

Excel deletes all autosaved files for a workbook after four days or if you save and close the workbook.

If you make changes to your workbook and attempt to close the file before saving the changes, Excel displays a message giving you the option to save or not save the file. In earlier versions of Excel, if you accidentally clicked the Don't Save button when you really wanted to save the workbook, all your changes were lost. In Excel 2010, if you close the workbook without saving changes, Excel retains the last autosaved version of the workbook, so you can recover your changes up to the last time AutoRecover saved the workbook. To open this version of the workbook, go Backstage and select the file on the Recent tab. The file has the following added descriptive label: *(when I closed without saving)*.

Reviewing Workbook Properties

Excel 2010's Backstage view consolidates all workbook properties, such as the workbook's location, author, and title, and when the workbook was created and last modified.

Click the File tab on the Ribbon to go to the Backstage view, and then click the Info tab in the Backstage navigation pane if it isn't already selected. At the top of the Info tab, Excel provides the full file path of the workbook. You can explore the options available for Permissions, Prepare for Sharing, and Versions by clicking the appropriate button and choosing an option from the menu.

The right side of the tab contains the following document-related categories:

- **Properties:** Displays a list of document information, most of which you can change by clicking the text box next to the property name. For example, to add a title, click the text that displays Add a title. Clicking the text exposes a text box in which you can enter a title. Click the Show All Properties link to display additional options.

- **Related Dates:** Displays a list of dates related to the document — the create date, the date last modified, and the date last printed.

- **Related People:** Displays a list of one or more authors who contributed to the document and the person who last modified the file. You can add a person to the list of authors. If other authors are in your Contacts list, you can click an author's name and select a contact method, if you need to contact the author.

- **Related Documents:** Click the Open File Location button if you want to open other workbooks stored in the same location as the active workbook.

Saving Workbooks

When you save a workbook, Excel saves the copy in memory to your drive — overwriting the previous copy of the workbook. When you save a workbook for the first time, Excel displays its Save As dialog box.

Excel 2010's native file format is based on a standard called Open XML (eXtensible Markup Language). XML is a text-based file format — older versions of Excel (before Excel 2007) used a binary file format.

You don't need to have knowledge of XML or Open XML to work in Excel. However, it is useful to know that Excel 2010, like earlier versions, saves files with a different file extension depending on the type of file you're saving. A list of typical file types and the extension names they use are in the following table. We also include the corresponding file extensions used in earlier versions of Excel.

File Type	2007+ Extension	Pre-2007 Extension
Excel workbook native format	.xlsx	.xls
Excel macro-enabled workbook	.xlsm	.xls
Excel workbook template	.xltx	.xlt
Excel macro-enabled workbook template	.xltm	.xlt
Excel binary workbook	.xlsb	.xls
Excel add-in	.xlam	.xla

Remember: Unlike earlier versions of Excel, Excel 2007 or later version workbooks or templates containing *macros* (scripts written to enhance Excel in some manner) are stored in files that differ from files without macros. If you attempt to save a macro-based workbook or template in a format that doesn't support macros (.xlsx or .xltx), Excel gives you the option to save the file without macros or to select a format that supports macros (.xlsm or .xltm).

Saving a workbook

Use any of the following methods to save the active workbook:

- ✔ Click the File tab on the Ribbon and then click Save.
- ✔ Click the Save button on the Quick Access toolbar.
- ✔ Press Ctrl+S.
- ✔ Press Shift+F12.

If the document you're saving does not yet have a name, Excel prompts you for a name by opening its Save As dialog box. You can give the document a name and navigate to the folder where you want to store the file. *See also* "Saving a workbook under a different name," in the next section.

Saving a workbook under a different name

Sometimes you may want to keep multiple versions of your work by saving each successive version under a different name.

To save a workbook with a different name, follow these steps:

1. Click the File tab on the Ribbon and then click Save As. Excel displays the Save As dialog box.

2. Windows XP: In the Save In drop-down list, select the folder in which to save the workbook.

   Windows Vista and Windows 7: Select the folder in which to save the workbook (see Figure 2-3).

3. In the File Name text box, enter a new filename. (You don't need to include a file extension.)

4. Click Save.

Figure 2-3

Excel creates a new copy of the workbook with a different name, but the original version of the workbook remains intact. (Note that the original workbook is no longer open.)

Saving a workbook in a non-native file format

To share a workbook with someone who uses an application that opens files in a format other than Excel 2010's native format, be sure to save the workbook in a file format that the other application can read.

Excel can save workbook contents in many non-Excel file formats, such as tab- or comma-delimited text, html, and standard xml.

To save a workbook in a different file format, follow these steps:

1. Click the File tab on the Ribbon and then click Save As. Excel displays the Save As dialog box.

2. In the Save As Type drop-down list, select the format in which you want to save the file. For example, to save in an earlier Excel file format, select Excel 97-2003 Workbook.

3. Click Save.

See also "Sharing Workbooks," next in this part.

Remember: If you attempt to save a workbook with features not supported in the file format you're saving to, Excel displays a warning message. If the format you're saving to is an earlier version of Excel, Excel displays the Compatibility Checker dialog box, which shows you a list of features that will be lost.

Sharing Workbooks

After you create and save a workbook you may want to share the workbook. If you're sharing the workbook with others in your internal computer network, you can simply save the file to a shared server folder with appropriate permissions set for users accessing the file.

Excel provides other methods to share a workbook, such as e-mailing it or saving it to SharePoint. Follow these steps to share a workbook:

1. Click the File tab on the Ribbon and then click the Save & Send tab in the Backstage navigation pane. The Save & Send tab contains additional tabs arranged in two categories: Save & Send and File Types. File Types provides a convenient list of common file types to which you can save your workbook before sharing.

2. Click a tab in the Save & Send category and select an option on the tab. For example, if you want to e-mail a file, click the Send Using E-mail tab and then click an e-mail option on the right side of the tab.

Switching among Open Workbooks

If you have multiple workbooks open, they usually appear maximized on-screen so that you can view only one workbook at a time.

To switch the active display among workbooks, use one of the following methods:

✔ Click the View tab on the Ribbon, click the Switch Windows button, and then select one of the workbook names on the menu that appears.

✔ Press Ctrl+F6 or Ctrl+Tab to cycle the active display among the open workbooks.

Working with Workbook Templates

A *workbook template* is basically a workbook that contains one or more worksheets set up with formatting and formulas and ready for you to enter data and get immediate results. A workbook template can use any of Excel's features, such as charts, formulas, and macros. Excel includes templates that automate the common tasks of filling in invoices, expense statements, and purchase orders. You can also download more templates from the Internet. You can also create your own templates from scratch or from an existing workbook.

Creating a workbook template

To save a workbook as a template, follow these steps:

1. Click the File tab on the Ribbon and then click Save As. Excel displays the Save As dialog box.

2. In the Save As Type drop-down list, select Excel Template.

3. If you want to save the template in a subfolder of the Templates folder in Windows XP: Excel displays the Templates folder in the Save In drop-down list. Select the subfolder in the Save In drop-down list.

   If you want to save the template in a subfolder of the Templates folder in Windows Vista or Windows 7: After you complete Step 2, Excel displays the Templates folder. Select a subfolder in the Templates folder.

If you select a subfolder in the Templates folder, it should be a subfolder that you've previously created. If you save the template in an Excel installed subfolder, the template will not appear when you want to create a workbook from the template.

To create a new folder in the Templates folder in which you can save the template, click the Create New Folder button (or the New Folder button) in the Save As dialog box and give the new folder a name.

4. In the File Name box, enter a name for the template, and then click Save. Excel saves templates with an .xltx file extension. If your template contains macros, Excel gives you the option to save the template without macros or to save in a format that supports macros (.xltm). *See also* "Saving Files," earlier in this part.

You can also save a template in an earlier file format. In Step 2, select Excel 97-2003 Template from the Save As Type drop-down list box.

To prevent overwriting the template file when you create a new workbook from a template, always save your templates in the Templates folder or a subfolder you create within the Templates folder. See also "Creating a workbook from a template," next.

Creating a workbook from a template

If you create a new workbook that you based on a template, Excel creates a copy of the template in memory so that the original template, on disk, remains intact. The default workbook name is the template name with a number appended to it. For example, if you create a new workbook based on a template by the name of Report.xltx, the workbook default name is Report1.xlsx. The first time that you save a workbook that you create from a template, Excel displays the Save As dialog box so that you can give the file a meaningful name.

To create a workbook from a template, follow these steps:

1. Click the File tab on the Ribbon and then click the New tab in the Backstage navigation pane. See Figure 2-4.

Figure 2-4

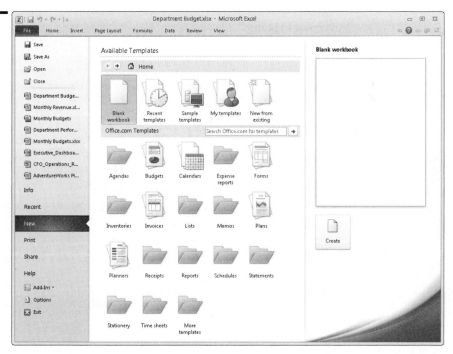

2. Select a template option on the New tab. The New tab is divided into two sections. The top section is for templates on your local computer, and the bottom section is for templates located at Office.com. The options in the top area are as follows:

   • **Recent templates:** Click the Recent templates button to display your recently used templates. If you have not yet created any templates, the list will be empty. Select a template and click Create to open a copy of the template file.

   • **Sample templates:** These are templates that are in your system when you install Excel. Click the Sample templates button to display a list of sample templates. Select a template and click Create to open a copy of the template.

   • **My templates:** These are templates you previously saved in the Templates folder or in a subfolder you create in the Templates folder. Click My templates to display the New dialog box. Templates you saved in the Templates folder appear in the Personal Templates tab. If you saved Templates in one or more subfolders that you previously created in the Templates folder, the folder names appear as tabs in the New dialog box. Select a template from a tab and click OK. Excel opens a copy of the template.

   • **New from existing:** This option allows you to use any workbook as a template or to use a template file that's not in the Templates folder. Click New from Existing to display the New from Existing Workbook dialog box. Navigate to the folder containing the file you want to use as a template, select the file in the folder, and click Create New. Excel opens a copy of the file.

   If you're connected to the Internet, you can select from one of the online categories at the bottom of the New tab. Click a template or click a folder and then click a template within the folder, click Download (or double-click the template), and Excel opens a copy of the template.

3. Save the workbook after you enter the appropriate data in the template copy. ***See also*** "Saving Workbooks" and "Creating a workbook template," earlier in this part.

Working with Worksheets

A workbook can consist of any number of *worksheets*. Each sheet has a tab that appears at the bottom of the workbook window. In this part, we discuss several useful things that you can do with worksheets.

In this part . . .

- ✔ **Adding and Deleting Worksheets**
- ✔ **Copying and Moving a Worksheet**
- ✔ **Changing a Worksheet's Name**
- ✔ **Hiding and Unhiding a Worksheet**
- ✔ **Protecting a Worksheet**
- ✔ **Zooming a Worksheet**

Activating a Worksheet

Before you can do any work in a worksheet, you must first activate it. To *activate* a worksheet, just click its tab. If the tab for the sheet that you want to activate isn't visible, use the tab scrolling buttons to scroll the sheet tabs. Figure 3-1 shows how Excel highlights the active sheet. You also can use the following shortcut keys to activate a different sheet:

  ✔ **Ctrl+PgUp:** Activates the previous sheet, if you have one.

  ✔ **Ctrl+PgDn:** Activates the next sheet, if you have one.

Figure 3-1

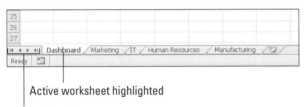

Active worksheet highlighted

Tab scrolling buttons

Adding a New Worksheet

You can add a new worksheet to a workbook in the following ways:

  ✔ Click the Insert Worksheet tab button, which is located after the last worksheet tab in the workbook.

  ✔ Right-click any sheet tab, choose Insert from the menu, and click Worksheet in the Insert dialog box. Click OK to insert the new worksheet.

  ✔ On the Ribbon's Home tab, click the arrow portion of the Insert button, and then choose Insert Sheet from the menu.

  ✔ Press Shift+F11.

In each case, Excel inserts a new worksheet and it becomes the active worksheet. The default name that Excel gives to the worksheet is the word *Sheet,* followed by a number (for example, Sheet1, Sheet2, and so on).

Changing a Worksheet's Name

By default, Excel names its worksheets Sheet1, Sheet2, and so on. Providing more meaningful names helps you identify a particular sheet. To change a sheet's name:

1. Double-click the sheet tab, or right-click the sheet tab and choose Rename from the menu that appears. Either method selects the text in the tab.

2. Type the new sheet name directly on the tab.

Remember: Sheet names can be up to 31 characters long. Names can include spaces but not the following characters: [ ] (brackets); : (colon); / (slash); \ (backslash); ? (question mark); and * (asterisk).

Coloring a Worksheet Tab

Excel lets you to add color to a worksheet tab. You can use this feature, for example, to quickly identify a specific worksheet by its color. To color a worksheet tab, follow these steps:

1. Right-click the sheet tab, and choose Tab Color from the menu that appears.

2. Select a color for the tab from the color picker that appears.

To undo the tab color, follow the same procedure, but in Step 2, click the No Color option in the color picker.

Remember: If you select a tab that you have color-coded, the tab color changes to a gradient fill, with a very light fill behind the sheet name. If a tab is fully colored, it's not currently selected.

Copying or Moving a Worksheet

Sometimes, you may want to rearrange the order of worksheets in a workbook, copy a worksheet within the same workbook or to a different workbook, or move a sheet to a different workbook. The procedures for copying and moving a worksheet are similar.

You can copy or move a worksheet in any of the following ways:

✔ **Copy or move using a dialog box:** Right-click the worksheet tab and choose Move or Copy from the menu that appears. Excel opens the Move or Copy dialog box, as shown in Figure 3-2. Select the location for the copy or move in the To Book drop-down list (to copy or move the sheet to a new or other open workbook) or the Before Sheet list box, or both. To *move* the sheet, *deselect* the Create a Copy check box, and click OK. To *copy* the sheet, *select* the Create a Copy check box, and click OK.

✔ **Copy using drag and drop:** Click the worksheet tab, press Ctrl, and drag the sheet to the desired location in the workbook. As you drag, the mouse pointer changes to a small sheet with a plus sign on it, and a small arrow guides you. To use this method to copy a worksheet to another open workbook, you must first arrange the workbooks. *See* "Arranging Windows Automatically," in Part 2.

✔ **Move using drag and drop:** Click the sheet tab, and drag the sheet to its desired location in the workbook. As you drag, the mouse pointer changes to a small sheet, and a small arrow guides you. To use this method to move a worksheet to another open workbook, you must first arrange the workbooks.

Figure 3-2

Remember: To copy or move a worksheet to a different workbook using any of the methods described, both workbooks must be open.

Remember: After you copy or move a worksheet (the source worksheet) to a different workbook, any defined names and custom formats used in the worksheet are copied to the new workbook. If one or more name conflicts exist between the destination workbook and the source worksheet, Excel may display a message giving you the option to either use the name(s) in the destination workbook or change the name(s) used in the source worksheet. You don't have the choice to use the name(s) in the source worksheet.

See also "Creating Names," in Part 6.

Deleting a Worksheet

To delete a worksheet, right-click the sheet tab and choose Delete from the menu that appears. If the sheet you want to delete contains data (or if you delete all the data on a sheet in the current session), Excel asks you to confirm the fact that you want to delete the sheet. Every workbook must contain at least one sheet, so if you try to delete the only sheet, Excel complains.

To select multiple sheets to delete, press Ctrl while clicking the sheet tabs that you want to delete. To select a group of contiguous sheets, click the first sheet tab, press Shift, and then click the last sheet tab.

 After you delete a worksheet, it's gone for good. This operation is one of the few in Excel that you can't undo. Therefore, you may want to save a workbook before deleting worksheets. Then, if you inadvertently delete a worksheet, you can revert to the saved version.

Freezing Row or Column Titles

Many worksheets are set up with row and column headings. As you scroll through such worksheets, you can easily get lost after the row and column headings scroll out of view. Excel provides a handy solution to alleviate this problem: you can freeze the rows and columns.

To freeze entire rows or columns, follow these steps:

1. Move the cell pointer to the cell *below* the row that you want to freeze and to the *right* of the column that you want to freeze. Use the following steps to freeze various portions of the worksheet:

   • To freeze row 1 and column A, for example, move the cell pointer to cell B2.

   • To freeze rows only, move the cell pointer below the rows that you want to freeze in column A.

   • To freeze columns only, move the cell pointer to the right of the columns that you want to freeze in row 1.

2. Click the View tab on the Ribbon.

3. Click the Freeze Panes button and choose Freeze Panes from the menu. Excel inserts dark lines in the worksheet to indicate the frozen rows and columns. These frozen rows and columns remain visible as you scroll throughout the worksheet.

To unfreeze the frozen rows or columns, repeat Steps 2 and 3, but in Step 3, choose Unfreeze Panes from the menu. *See also* "Splitting Panes," later in this part.

 You can quickly freeze the top row or left column by clicking the View tab on the Ribbon, clicking the Freeze Panes button, and choosing either Freeze Top Row or Freeze First Column from the menu. These options are useful because data is often stored in worksheets with labels in the top row, or the first column, or both. Note that the cell pointer can be in any location when you select these options.

 An alternative to freezing row and column titles is to convert the range to a table. When table headers scroll off the sheet, Excel displays the header titles in the column header area. *See* Part 11, "Working with Tables."

Grouping and Ungrouping Worksheets

Excel allows you to group multiple worksheets so that you can perform tasks on all the sheets in the group simultaneously. For example, you can group sheets to print, you can apply formatting to a given range in all the sheets in a group, or you can enter data into the same cell or range in all the sheets in the group. Any modifications you make to one sheet in the group are applied to the other sheets in the group.

Grouping worksheets

If the sheets you want to group are contiguous (adjacent), follow these steps:

1. Select the tab of the first sheet by clicking it.

2. Press and hold down the Shift key and select the tab of the last sheet. Excel selects all the sheets between the first and last, inclusive.

If the sheets you want to group are not contiguous, follow these steps:

1. Select the tab of the first sheet by clicking it.

2. Press and hold down the Ctrl key and click the tabs of the other sheets in turn.

Remember: You can't switch among sheets in a group if all the sheets in the workbook are grouped. In this case, clicking any *inactive* sheet tab (any sheet tab with the name not highlighted) ungroups all the worksheets.

 If you need to group and switch among all your existing worksheets in the workbook, add a new (blank) worksheet first. *See also* "Adding a New Worksheet," earlier in this part.

Ungrouping worksheets

You can use any of the following methods to ungroup worksheets. The first three methods ungroup all worksheets; the last ungroups only an inactive sheet.

✔ Click any unselected sheet tab to ungroup all worksheets.

✔ Press and hold down the Shift key and click the *active* sheet tab (the sheet tab with the highlighted name) to ungroup all worksheets.

✔ If all the sheets in the workbook are grouped, click any *inactive* sheet tab to ungroup all worksheets.

✔ Press and hold down the Ctrl key and click an *inactive* sheet tab in the group to ungroup only that worksheet.

Hiding and Unhiding a Worksheet

Hiding a worksheet is useful if you don't want others to see it or if you just want to get it out of the way. If a sheet is hidden, its sheet tab is also hidden.

To hide a worksheet, right-click the worksheet tab and choose Hide from the contextual menu.

You can select multiple sheets to hide at once. If the sheets you want to hide are contiguous, click the first sheet, press and hold down Shift, and click the last sheet. If the sheets are noncontiguous, click the first sheet, press and hold down Ctrl, and click the other sheets in succession.

Remember: Every workbook must have at least one visible sheet, so Excel doesn't allow you to hide all sheets in a workbook.

To unhide a hidden worksheet, follow these steps:

1. Right-click any visible sheet tab and click Unhide from the contextual menu, or click the View tab on the Ribbon and click the Unhide button. Excel displays the Unhide dialog box.

2. Select the sheet that you want to unhide and click OK. You can unhide only one sheet at a time.

TIP

To prevent someone from unhiding a worksheet, you can protect the workbook. **See** "Protecting and unprotecting a workbook structure or window," in Part 2.

Protecting a Worksheet

Deleting a single formula in a worksheet often creates a ripple effect, causing other formulas to produce an error value or, even worse, incorrect results. You can circumvent such problems by locking the cells that you don't want to be modified and then protecting your worksheets from modification. Follow these steps:

1. Right-click the tab of the worksheet you want to protect and choose Protect Sheet from the contextual menu, or click the Review tab on the Ribbon and click the Protect Sheet button. The Protect Sheet dialog box appears, as shown in Figure 3-3.

Figure 3-3

2. Provide a password in the Protect Sheet dialog box, if you want.

   • If you enter a password, you must reenter the password before the sheet can be unprotected.

   • If you don't supply a password, anyone can unprotect the sheet.

3. In the Allow All Users of This Worksheet To list box, click the appropriate check boxes to select the elements that users can change after the sheet is protected.

4. Click OK.

Remember: By default, the locked property is turned on for all cells and objects, which means that they are locked when you protect the worksheet. Before protecting a worksheet, you normally want to unlock the input cells (the cells in which you enter data). To lock or unlock cells, first select them, and then right-click and choose Format Cells from the contextual menu; then check or uncheck the Lock check box on the Protection tab. **See also** "Selecting Cells and Ranges," in Part 4.

To remove protection from a protected sheet, right-click the worksheet you want to unprotect and choose Unprotect Sheet from the contextual menu, or click the Review tab on the Ribbon and click the Unprotect Sheet button. If the sheet was protected with a password, you have to enter the password before you can unprotect the sheet.

Splitting Panes

Splitting an Excel window into two or four panes enables you to view multiple parts of the same worksheet. Some of the key features of splitting panes are as follows:

   ✔ Clicking the View tab on the Ribbon and then clicking the Split button splits the active worksheet into two or four separate panes.

 ✔ The split occurs at the location of the cell pointer.

 ✔ You can use the mouse to drag and resize the pane.

 ✔ To remove the split panes, click the View tab on the Ribbon and then click the Split button.

A faster way to split and unsplit panes is to drag the vertical or horizontal split bar, as shown in Figure 3-4. These split bars are standard elements of the Excel window and are located above and to the right of the vertical and horizontal scroll bars, respectively. To remove split panes by using the mouse, drag the pane separator all the way to the edge of the window or just double-click it.

Figure 3-4

	Customer	Customer Type	ShipTo City	ShipTo State	Region	Account	Total Commission	Commission Paid Date
6	Company L	COL	COLUMBIA	SC	SE	COL-SE	$2.47	26-Jan-07
7	Company L	COL	COLUMBIA	SC	SE	COL-SE	$2.10	26-Jan-07
8	Company L	COL	MONTGOMERY	AL	SE	COL-SE	$366.93	26-Jan-07
9	Company L	COL	MONTGOMERY	AL	SE	COL-SE	$141.36	26-Jan-07
10	Company L	COL	MONTGOMERY	AL	SE	COL-SE	$93.90	26-Jan-07
11	Company L	COL	MONTGOMERY	AL	SE	COL-SE	$37.87	26-Jan-07
12	Company L	COL	N CHARLESTON	SC	SE	COL-SE	$13.02	26-Jan-07
13	Company L	COL	N CHARLESTON	SC	SE	COL-SE	$12.78	26-Jan-07
14	Company BC	COBC	LINCOLN	NE	CENTRAL	COBC-CENTRAL	$73.36	26-Jan-07
15	Company U	COU	ATLANTA	GA	SE	SE	$119.44	26-Jan-07
16	Company AG	COAG	JACKSON	MS	SE	SE	$31.86	26-Jan-07
17	Company AG	COAG	JACKSON	MS	SE	SE	$2.00	26-Jan-07
51	Company L	COL	TALLAHASSEE	FL	SE	COL-SE	$9.47	26-Jan-07
52	Company L	COL	TALLAHASSEE	FL	SE	COL-SE	$2.02	26-Jan-07
53	Company C	T2	ATLANTA	GA	SE	SE	$7.12	26-Jan-07
54	Company U	COU	MEMPHIS	TN	SE	SE	$59.80	26-Jan-07
55	Company U	COU	JACKSON	TN	SE	SE	$28.52	26-Jan-07
56	Company BC	COBC	LEXINGTON	KY	SE	COBC-SE	$47.76	26-Jan-07
57	Company BC	COBC	LEXINGTON	KY	SE	COBC-SE	$10.08	26-Jan-07
58	Company U	COU	GAINESVILLE	GA	SE	SE	$30.68	26-Jan-07
59	Company C	T2	ATLANTA	GA	SE	SE	$7.92	26-Jan-07
60	Company U	COU	LOUISVILLE	KY	SE	SE	$30.68	26-Jan-07
61	Company U	COU	LOUISVILLE	KY	SE	SE	$28.96	26-Jan-07
62	Company U	COU	LOUISVILLE	KY	SE	SE	$28.92	26-Jan-07
63	Company U	COU	LOUISVILLE	KY	SE	SE	$30.30	26-Jan-07
64	Company L	COL	TAMPA	FL	SE	COL-SE	$5.98	26-Jan-07
65	Company L	COL	TAMPA	FL	SE	COL-SE	$4.40	26-Jan-07
66	Company L	COL	BIRMINGHAM	AL	SE	COL-SE	$19.66	26-Jan-07
67	Company L	COL	BIRMINGHAM	AL	SE	COL-SE	$19.62	26-Jan-07
68	Company L	COL	TALLAHASSEE	FL	SE	COL-SE	$2.81	9-Feb-07
69	Company L	COL	TALLAHASSEE	FL	SE	COL-SE	$1.46	9-Feb-07
70	Company L	COL	TALLAHASSEE	FL	SE	COL-SE	$1.47	9-Feb-07
71	Company L	COL	DAYTONA BEACH	FL	SE	COL-SE	$1.49	9-Feb-07
72	Company L	COL	DAYTONA BEACH	FL	SE	COL-SE	$1.46	9-Feb-07

Sales Commissions DEMO.xlsm — Procedure / Master / Commission Structure

See also "Freezing Row or Column Titles," earlier in this part.

Turning Off Gridlines

Sometimes you're working with data to which you've applied a number of formatting options, but you find the worksheet gridlines distracting. To turn off the gridline display, click the View tab on the Ribbon and then click to clear the Gridlines check box.

Remember: Whether or not you have the gridline display turned on, gridlines aren't printed unless you select that option in the Sheet Options group on the Ribbon's Page Layout tab. *See also* "Printing gridlines or row and column headings," in Part 9.

Using Full-Screen View

If you want to see as much information as possible in a worksheet, you can hide the Ribbon controls or choose a full-screen view:

🖝 **See** "Hiding the Ribbon commands," in Part 1.

🖝 Click the View tab on the Ribbon and then click the Full Screen button. The Ribbon and its tabs, the Quick Access toolbar, the formula bar, and the status bar all disappear. Press Esc to restore the hidden elements.

Zooming a Worksheet

Excel enables you to scale the size of your worksheets from 10 percent to 400 percent. Using a low zoom percentage can help you get a bird's-eye view of your worksheet to see its layout. A high zoom percentage can help you decipher very small text.

The easiest way to change the zoom factor of the active worksheet is to use the zoom control at the bottom right of the status bar (see Figure 3-5). You can drag the slider to zoom in and out or you can click the Zoom in (+) or Zoom out (–) buttons to change the view by 10 percent (per each click). The button on the immediate left of the Zoom out button displays the current zoom percentage. Clicking this button displays the Zoom dialog box. (You can open the Zoom dialog box also by clicking the View tab on the Ribbon and then clicking the Zoom button.)

Figure 3-5

 TIP The Zoom dialog box is useful if you want to use a precise zoom level (by entering a value in the custom box) or zoom a selection — for example, a selected range of cells or chart, to fit the worksheet window (by selecting the Fit Selection option).

 FAST TRACK If you have a Microsoft IntelliMouse or equivalent device (generally, any mouse with a scroll wheel), you can zoom in or out in a worksheet by pressing Ctrl while you roll the mouse wheel. If this feature is not working, make sure that the Zoom on Roll with IntelliMouse option is selected in the Excel Options dialog box. (Click the File tab and then click the Options button. Click the Advanced category, and in the Editing Options section, select the Zoom on Roll with IntelliMouse check box.)

Entering and Editing Worksheet Data

This part deals with two of the most common tasks you're likely to perform on a daily basis in Excel: entering data into worksheet cells and editing (or changing) the data after you enter it. Excel provides many handy tools to make these tasks painless and efficient.

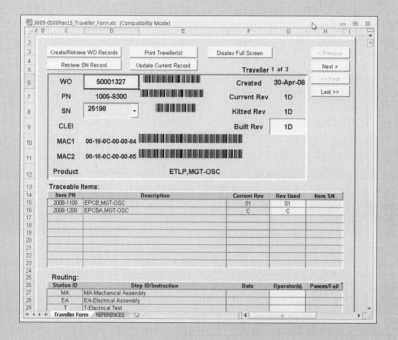

In this part . . .

- ✔ Copying Cells and Ranges
- ✔ Editing the Contents of a Cell
- ✔ Entering Dates, Formulas, Text, and Values
- ✔ Undoing Changes and Mistakes
- ✔ Validating Data Entry

Copying Cells and Ranges

Copying cells is a common spreadsheet operation, and several types of copying are possible. You can do any of the following:

- ✔ Copy one cell to another cell.

- ✔ Copy a cell to a range of cells. Excel copies the source cell to every cell in the destination range.

- ✔ Copy a range to another range.

- ✔ Copy multiple cells or ranges to another range.

A copy procedure is really a combination of two operations: a copy operation, which copies the cell contents to the *Windows Clipboard,* followed by a paste operation, which places the contents of the Clipboard into the destination cell or range.

When you paste the contents of the Clipboard to the destination cell or range, Excel provides you with several paste options. For example, you can paste all contents, formulas, formatting, and comments (if any) that were applied to the original cell or range (this is the default paste operation). Alternatively, you can select from among different combinations of formula, value, and formatting options.

Excel 2010 introduces a new Paste Options gallery, which replaces the textual paste options list in earlier versions of the product. The gallery consists of a series of icons, each of which represents one or more combinations of paste options. The gallery shows up in three locations — under the Paste button on the Ribbon's Home tab, in the right-click contextual menu, and in the Paste Options Smart Tag. See Figure 4-1.

Like many other features in Excel 2010, the Paste Options gallery provides a live preview — you can hover the mouse cursor over a paste option to see what the results will be *before* committing to an option.

Copying a cell to another cell or a range

To copy the contents of one cell to a range of cells, follow these steps:

Figure 4-1

Paste Options
gallery on
the Ribbon

Paste Options gallery
on the right-click menu

Paste Options
gallery in the
Smart Tag

1. Move the cell pointer to the cell that you want to copy (the source cell).

2. Click the Copy button on the Ribbon's Home tab. (You can also press Ctrl+C or right-click the cell and choose Copy from the contextual menu.)

3. Select the cell or range that you want to hold the copy (the destination cell or range).

4. To select the default paste operation, click the top part of the Paste split button on the Ribbon's Home tab. Alternatively, you can press Ctrl+V or right-click the destination cell or range and choose the leftmost icon immediately below the Paste Options label on the contextual menu.

To select another paste option, click the arrow part of the Paste split button, and hover the mouse cursor over the icons in the gallery to preview your choices. In addition to the live preview, Excel displays a ScreenTip for each icon that provides descriptive text to help you with your choice.

As an alternative to using the Paste button on the Ribbon to select another paste option, you can right-click the destination cell or range and hover over the available choices in the contextual menu. The menu displays the most common paste options. To view additional choices, select Paste Special and hover over the options in the flyout gallery.

5. After you make a selection, Excel displays the Paste Options Smart Tag next to the copied range. Clicking the Smart Tag, or pressing Ctrl, displays a gallery of alternative paste options, as shown in Figure 4-1. The Smart Tag options are handy if you want to change your paste option after the fact.

   If you don't need to change your paste option, you can press Enter or Esc to dismiss the Smart Tag.

 If the range you're copying to is adjacent to the cell you're copying from, you can drag the cell's AutoFill handle to copy the cell to the adjacent range. Note, however, that Excel provides far fewer paste options if you use the AutoFill method. **See** "Filling a Series," later in this part.

Copying a range to another range

To copy the contents of one range to another range of the same size, follow these steps:

1. Select the range that you want to copy.

2. Click the Copy button on the Ribbon's Home tab. (You can also press Ctrl+C or right-click the range and choose Copy from the contextual menu.)

3. Select only the upper-left cell of the range that you want to use to hold the copy.

4. Complete Steps 4 and 5 in the section "Copying a cell to another cell or a range," immediately preceding in this part.

 If you intend to use the default paste option and you decide that the location you're copying to isn't too far away, you can follow these steps:

1. Select the cell or range to copy.

2. Press and hold down Ctrl.

3. Move the mouse pointer to any of the selection's borders. The mouse pointer changes to an arrow with a small plus sign.

4. Drag the mouse to the location where you want to copy the cell or range. Excel displays an outline of the range as you drag with the mouse to help you see where you're going to paste the range.

5. Release the mouse button. Excel copies the cell or range to the new location.

Remember: If the mouse pointer doesn't change to an arrow in Step 3, your drag-and-drop feature is off. To turn on the drag-and-drop feature, follow these steps:

1. Click the File tab and then click the Options button.

2. In the Excel Options dialog box, click the Advanced category.

3. In the Editing options section, select the Enable Fill Handle and Cell Drag-and-Drop check box.

4. To prevent accidental overwriting of data in the destination range, select the Alert before Overwriting Cells check box.

5. Click OK.

Copying data to another worksheet or workbook

To copy the contents of a cell or range to another worksheet or workbook, follow these steps:

1. Select the cell or range that you want to copy.

2. Click the Copy button on the Ribbon's Home tab. (You can also press Ctrl+C or right-click the cell or range and choose Copy from the contextual menu.)

3. Click the tab of the worksheet that you're copying to. If the worksheet is in a different workbook, activate that workbook (by clicking the View tab on the Ribbon, clicking the Switch Windows button, and selecting the workbook name from the menu) and then click the tab of the worksheet that will hold the copied data.

4. Select only the upper-left cell of the range that will hold the copy.

5. Complete Steps 4 and 5 in the section "Copying a cell to another cell or a range," earlier in this part.

Copying multiple cells or ranges to another range

To copy noncontiguous cells or ranges to a single range elsewhere in the worksheet, to a different worksheet in the same workbook, or to a range in a different workbook, you can copy and paste each cell or range in turn to the new range. However, Excel provides a simpler and less tedious method to perform this multiple-copy task. This method uses the *Office Clipboard* to copy multiple data items before pasting the items. The Office Clipboard differs from the Windows Clipboard in that the Windows Clipboard can store data from a *single* copy operation at a time.

The Office Clipboard can store 24 copied items. All Office applications share a single Office Clipboard, enabling you to cut and paste multiple items between Excel and other Office applications, such as Word and PowerPoint.

To copy multiple cells or ranges to another range, follow these steps:

1. Select the Home tab on the Ribbon if it isn't already selected and click the Clipboard group dialog launcher button, located on the bottom right of the group container. Excel displays the *Clipboard task pane,* as shown in Figure 4-2.

Figure 4-2

2. Select the first cell or range that you want to copy. (**See** "Selecting Cells and Ranges," later in this part.)

3. Click the Copy button on the Ribbon's Home tab. (You can also press Ctrl+C or right-click the cell or range and choose Copy from the contextual menu.) Excel copies the data to the Office Clipboard. The Clipboard task pane displays all or a portion of the copied data.

4. Select the next cell or range that you want to copy. (The cell or range can be from the same worksheet, another worksheet in the same workbook, or a worksheet in another open workbook.)

5. Repeat Steps 3 and 4 for all the remaining data that you want to copy.

6. Select the upper-left cell of the range that will hold the copied items.

7. Click the Paste All button in the Clipboard task pane. You can also click individual items in the Clipboard task pane to paste a single item at a time.

 You can enable the Office Clipboard by setting the Clipboard task pane to appear automatically after the second use of the Copy command. This option, if set, eliminates Steps 1 and 2. To turn on this option, click the Options button at the bottom of the Clipboard task pane and select the Show Office Clipboard Automatically option.

 Normally, you need to display the Clipboard task pane to enable the Office Clipboard. If you prefer to use the Office Clipboard without displaying the Clipboard task pane, click the Options button at the bottom of the Clipboard task pane and select the Collect Without Showing Office Clipboard option.

Remember: You can use the Office Clipboard for multiple cut operations in addition to the multiple copy operations that we discuss in this section.

Deleting Entire Rows and Columns

In certain circumstances, you may want to delete entire rows or columns from your worksheet. If you delete a row(s), the rows below the deleted row(s) shift upward to fill the gap. If you delete a column(s), the columns to the right of the deleted column(s) shift to the left to fill the gap.

To delete entire rows or columns, follow these steps:

1. Select the row header or column header of the row or column you want to delete. *See* "Selecting entire rows and columns," later in this part. Excel selects the entire row or column.

2. Use any of the following methods to delete the row or column:

- Right-click the selected row or column and choose Delete from the contextual menu.

- Press Ctrl+– (the minus sign).

- Click the upper portion of the Delete button on the Ribbon's Home tab (the portion above the button's name).

 Make sure that any cells that you want to keep aren't in the rows or columns you delete. You can zoom out in your worksheet to check for any cells that aren't normally visible on-screen. *See also* "Zooming a Worksheet," in Part 3.

Editing the Contents of a Cell

After you enter information into a cell, you can edit it. To edit the contents of a cell, use one of the following ways to get into cell-edit mode:

✔ Double-click the cell to edit the cell contents directly in the cell.

✔ Click the cell and press F2 to edit the cell contents directly in the cell.

✔ Click the cell that you want to edit; then click the formula bar to edit the cell contents in the formula bar.

All these methods cause the formula bar to display two new mouse icons. The following table describes these icons and what they do.

Icon	What It Does
✕	Cancels editing, and the cell's contents don't change. (Pressing Esc has the same effect.)
✓	Confirms the editing and enters the modified contents into the cell. (Pressing Enter has the same effect.)

Remember: If nothing happens after you double-click a cell, or if pressing F2 puts the cursor in the formula bar instead of directly in the cell, the in-cell editing feature is turned off. To turn on in-cell editing, follow these steps:

1. Click the File tab, and then click the Options button.

2. In the Excel Options dialog box, click the Advanced category.

3. In the Editing options section, select the Allow Editing Directly in the Cells check box.

4. Click OK.

If you're editing a cell that contains a formula, the name box (at the extreme left in the formula bar) displays a list of worksheet functions if you click the downward-pointing arrow next to the box. You can select a function from the list, and Excel provides assistance entering the arguments. The example in Figure 4-3 shows the contents of cell A1 after you double-click the cell for editing.

Figure 4-3

If you're editing the contents of a cell (either directly in the cell or in the formula bar), the cursor changes to a vertical bar; you can move the vertical bar by using the direction keys. You can add new characters at the cursor's location. After you're in edit mode, you can use any of the following keys or key combinations to perform your edits:

- ✔ **Left arrow/right arrow:** Moves the cursor left or right one character, respectively, without deleting any characters.

- ✔ **Ctrl+left arrow/Ctrl+right arrow:** Moves the cursor one group of characters to the left or right, respectively.

- ✔ **Shift+left arrow/ Shift+right arrow:** Selects characters to the left or right of the cursor, respectively.

- ✔ **Shift+Home:** Selects from the cursor to the first character in the cell.

- ✔ **Shift+End:** Selects from the cursor to the last character in the cell.

- ✔ **Backspace:** Erases the character to the immediate left of the cursor.

- ✔ **Delete:** Erases the character to the right of the cursor or erases all selected characters.

✔ **Insert:** Places Excel in ovr (overtype) mode. Rather than adding characters to the cell, you *overtype,* or replace, existing characters with new ones, depending on the position of the cursor.

✔ **Home:** Moves the cursor to the beginning of the cell entry.

✔ **End:** Moves the cursor to the end of the cell entry.

✔ **Enter:** Accepts the edited data.

 Remember: If you change your mind after editing a cell, you can click the undo button on the Quick Access toolbar (or press Ctrl+Z) to restore the cell's previous contents.

 You can use the mouse to select characters while you're editing a cell. Just click and drag the mouse pointer over the characters that you want to select.

Remember: If the cell is locked and the worksheet is protected, you can't make any changes to the cell unless you unprotect the worksheet. *See* "Protecting a Worksheet," in Part 3.

Entering Data into a Range

Excel provides timesaving methods for you to enter data quickly in a range of cells. These methods are particularly helpful if you need to enter a lot of data manually.

Entering data into a specific range

If you're entering data into a range of cells, you may want to select the entire range of cells before you start entering data. This action causes Excel to move the cell pointer to the next cell in the selection after you press Enter.

The procedure works as follows:

✔ If the selection consists of multiple rows, Excel moves down the column; after it reaches the end of the column, it moves to the top of the next column.

✔ To skip a cell, press Enter without entering anything.

✔ To back up a row, press Shift+Enter. If you prefer to enter the data by rows rather than by columns, press Tab. To back up a column, press Shift+Tab.

Entering the same data into a range of cells

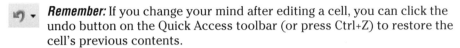 If you need to enter the same data (value, text, or formula) into multiple cells, your first inclination may be to enter it once and then copy it to the remaining cells. The following steps show you a better way:

1. Select all the cells that you want to contain the data. (**See** "Selecting a range," later in this part.)

2. Enter the value, text, or formula into the active cell in the range. This cell is already selected when you highlight the range.

3. Press Ctrl+Enter. Excel inserts the single entry into each cell in the selection.

Entering Dates and Times

Excel treats a date or a time as a value, but you format it to appear as a date or a time. If you work with dates and times, you need to understand Excel's date and time system.

Excel's system for working with dates uses a serial number system. The earliest date that Excel understands is January 1, 1900 (which has a serial number of 1). All other dates are counted from January 1, 1900. January 2, 1900 has a serial number of 2, January 1, 2010 has a serial number of 40179, and so on. Time is represented as a fraction of a day. For example, January 1, 2010 at 12:00:00 pm has a serial number of 40179.50. This system makes it easy to deal with dates and times in formulas.

Entering specific dates and times

Normally, you don't need to concern yourself with the Excel serial-number date system. You can simply enter a date in a familiar format, and Excel takes care of the details.

If you plan to use dates in formulas, make sure that the date you enter is one that Excel recognizes as a date (that is, a value); otherwise, your formula produces incorrect results. Excel is quite smart in recognizing dates that you enter into a cell, and it recognizes most common date formats. But it's not perfect. Excel interprets the following entries, for example, as text and not dates:

- ✔ June 1 2010
- ✔ Jun-1 2010
- ✔ Jun-1/2010

Remember: Excel uses a *windowing* approach for interpreting two-digit year entries. That is, within a 100-year window, Excel interprets 1/1/29 as January 1, 2029. If you enter 1/1/30, Excel interprets it as January 1, 1930. To be safe, enter the year as a four-digit value and then format it as you want.

The best way to deal with times is to enter the time into a cell in a recognized format. The following table lists some examples of time formats that Excel recognizes.

Entered into a Cell	Excel's Internal Interpretation
11:30:00 am	11:30 a.m.
11:30:00 AM	11:30 a.m.
11:30 pm	11:30 p.m.
11:30	11:30 a.m.

You also can combine dates and times, as follows.

Entered into a Cell	Excel's Internal Interpretation
January 1, 2010 12:00:00 pm	12:00 p.m. on January 1, 2010
6/1/10 11:30	11:30 a.m. on June 1, 2010

Entering the current date or time

If you need to date-stamp or time-stamp a cell in your worksheet, Excel provides the following two shortcut keys that perform this task for you:

- **Current date:** Press Ctrl+; (semicolon)
- **Current time:** Press Ctrl+Shift+; (semicolon)

Entering Formulas

A *formula* is a special type of cell entry that returns a result: After you enter a formula into a cell, the cell displays the result of the formula. The formula itself appears in the formula bar (which is just below the Ribbon) after you activate the cell.

A formula begins with an equal sign (=) and can consist of any of the following elements:

- Operators, such as + (for addition) and * (for multiplication)
- Cell references, including addresses such as B4 or C12, as well as named cells and ranges
- Values and text
- Worksheet functions (such as SUM)

You can enter a formula into a cell in one of two ways: manually (by typing it in) or by pointing to cell references. ***See also*** "Basic Formula Essentials," in Part 5, for more information on operators and operator precedence.

Entering formulas manually

To enter a formula manually, follow these steps:

1. Move the cell pointer (by clicking the cell with the mouse pointer or navigating with the arrow keys) to the cell that you want to hold the formula.

2. Type an equal sign (=) to signal the fact that the cell contains a formula.

3. Type the formula and press Enter.

As you type, a drop-down list appears below the cell. This is Excel's Formula AutoComplete feature. The feature tries to anticipate what you're typing and presents a list of matched items, as shown in Figure 4-4.

Figure 4-4

To select an item from the list, simply double-click the item or press the Tab key and Excel inserts the item in the formula.

Here are the types of items that appear in the Formula AutoComplete drop-down list:

- ✔ Excel built-in functions: All functions in the Excel library. **See also** "Entering functions manually," in Part 5.

- ✔ User-defined functions: Custom functions that supplement Excel's built-in functions through add-ins or through functions defined in the workbook (using Excel's macro language.)

- ✔ Defined names: All names you define in the workbook. **See also** Part 6, "Creating and Using Names."

- ✔ Table names: The names of all Tables in the workbook. **See also** Part 11, "Working with Tables."

The characters you type appear in the cell as well as in the formula bar. When entering a formula, you can use all the normal editing keys (Delete, Backspace, direction keys, and so on).

As you enter a formula, Excel shows each cell reference in the formula in a different color. If the reference cells are visible on the worksheet, you see a border around each cell in the same color as the cell reference in the formula. This feature makes it easier to identify the references of the cells you're typing in your formulas.

See also "Entering formulas by pointing," immediately following in this section.

If you find the Formula AutoComplete feature distracting, or you simply want to disable it temporarily, follow these steps to turn off the feature:

1. Click the File tab, and then click the Options button.

2. In the Excel Options dialog box, click the Formulas category.

3. In the Working with formulas section, deselect the Formula AutoComplete check box.

4. Click OK.

Entering formulas by pointing

The pointing method of entering a formula still involves some manual typing. The advantage is that you don't need to type the cell or range references. Instead, you point to them in the worksheet using the mouse or the arrow keys, which is usually more accurate and less tedious.

The best way to explain this procedure is with an example. Follow these steps to enter the formula **=A1/A2** into cell A3 by using the pointing method:

1. In cell A1, type **12000** and press Enter. In cell A2, type **240** and press Enter.

2. Move the cell pointer to cell A3 (by clicking the cell or navigating with the arrow keys). This cell is where you want the formula (and the result) to go.

3. Type an equal sign (=) to begin the formula.

4. Click cell A1 or press the up-arrow key twice. Note that Excel displays a moving border around the reference cell (A1) and the cell reference appears in cell A3 and in the formula bar (see Figure 4-5).

Figure 4-5

	A	B	C	D
1	12000			
2	240			
3	=A1			
4				

AVERAGE × ✓ f_x =A1

Excel colors the cell reference in the formula and the moving border around the reference cell (A1) with the same color.

5. Type a division sign (/). Excel now displays a solid-colored border around the A1 cell reference.

6. Click cell A2 or press the up-arrow key once. Excel adds A2 to the formula. Excel now displays a different color for the new cell reference in the formula and the same color for the border of the new reference cell.

7. Press Enter to end the formula entry.

See also "Entering formulas manually," earlier in this part.

Entering Text

You can use text in worksheets to serve as labels for values and headings for columns, or to provide instructions about the worksheet. An entry of mixed text and numbers is still considered text. A cell can hold as many as 32,767 characters.

Entering text into cells

To enter text (rather than a value or a formula) in a cell, follow these steps:

1. Move the cell pointer to the appropriate cell (by clicking the cell with the mouse pointer or by navigating with the arrow keys).

2. Type the text.

3. Press Enter or any of the direction keys.

If you enter text that's longer than the column's current width, one of the following happens:

- If the cells to the immediate right are blank, Excel displays the text in its entirety, spilling the entry into adjacent cells.

- If an adjacent cell isn't blank, Excel displays as much of the text as possible. (The cell contains the full text; it just doesn't display all of it.)

In either case, you can always see the text (as you type it and after you type it) because it appears in the formula bar as well as in the cell.

Note that the formula bar has its own space that never overlaps with the worksheet grid. By default, the formula bar displays a cell's contents on one line. If the cell contents exceeds the display capacity of a single line on the formula bar, Excel adds scroll arrows on the formula bar, as shown in Figure 4-6. You can view multiple lines of a cell's contents on the formula bar (one line at a time) by clicking the up or down scroll arrows.

If you want to keep multiple lines of a cell's content in view on the formula bar, you can adjust the height of the formula bar by dragging the resize bar at the bottom of the formula bar. As you drag the resize bar downwards, the worksheet grid is pushed down to accommodate the expanded formula bar. Clicking the Auto expand/collapse button at the far right of the formula bar (or pressing Ctrl+Shift+U) toggles between a single-line display and an expanded-line display (based on the last drag setting.)

Auto expand button

Figure 4-6

Resize cursor Resize bar Scroll arrows

Remember: To display a long text entry that's adjacent to a cell that contains an entry, you can edit your text to make it shorter, increase the width of the column, or wrap the text within the cell so that it occupies more than one line. **See also** "Modifying Cell Size," in Part 8.

Completing text entries by using AutoComplete

If you're entering a lot of repeated text entries into a column, AutoComplete can help you speed up the process. You type the first few letters of a text entry into a cell, and Excel automatically completes the entry based on other entries you've made in the column. Your column entries must be contiguous (that is, have no blank cells between entries). AutoComplete doesn't work with entries in a row.

AutoComplete works with no effort on your part; just follow these steps:

1. Begin entering text or a value. If Excel recognizes your entry, it automatically completes it.

2. If Excel guesses correctly, press Enter to accept it. To enter something else instead, just continue typing and ignore Excel's guess.

You can access this feature also by right-clicking the cell and choosing Pick from Drop-down List. If you use this method, Excel displays a list of all the entries in the current column. Just click the one you want, and Excel enters it automatically.

Remember: AutoComplete works only with pure text or mixed text (text and values); it doesn't work with pure values.

Entering Values

Values, also known as numbers, represent a quantity of some type: revenue, number of units, test scores, and so on. Values can stand on their own, or you can use the values you enter into cells as part of a formula or in creating a chart. Excel's numbers are precise up to 15 significant digits. If you enter a larger number, Excel stores it with only 15 digits of precision.

Entering values into cells

To enter a numeric value into a cell, follow these steps:

1. Move the cell pointer to the appropriate cell (by clicking the mouse pointer in the cell or by navigating with the arrow keys).

2. Enter the value.

3. Press Enter, Tab, or any of the direction keys. The value is displayed in the cell and also appears in the formula bar.

You can also include a decimal point, dollar sign, plus sign, minus sign, and comma. If you precede a value with a minus sign or enclose it in parentheses, Excel considers the value a negative number.

Remember: Sometimes the value doesn't appear exactly as you enter it. Excel may convert very large numbers to scientific notation. The formula bar, however, always displays the value that you originally entered.

Entering fractions

To enter a fraction into a cell, leave a space between the whole number part and the fractional part. To enter the decimal equivalent of 6⅞, for example, follow these steps:

1. Type **6**.

2. Type a space.

3. Type **7/8**.

4. Press Enter. Excel displays 6 7/8 in the cell and 6.875 in the formula bar. In addition, Excel sets the cell format as Fraction. *See also* "Formatting a Number," in Part 8.

If the value has no whole number part (for example, ⅛), you must enter a 0 and a space first, as follows: **0 1/8**. Otherwise, Excel interprets the entry as January 8 of the current year.

Erasing Data in Cells and Ranges

To erase the contents of a cell but leave the cell's formatting and cell comments intact, perform the following two steps:

1. Select the cell or range that you want to erase. (**See** "Selecting Cells and Ranges," later in this part, for details.)

2. Press Delete.

For more control over what you delete, click the Clear button on the Ribbon's Home tab and select an option from the menu. The menu contains the following six choices:

- ✔ **Clear All:** Clears everything from the cell or range

- ✔ **Clear Formats:** Clears only the formatting in the cell or range, and leaves the value, text, or formula

- ✔ **Clear Contents:** Clears only the cell's or range's contents and leaves the formatting

- ✔ **Clear Comments:** Clears the comment(s) attached to the cell or range (if a comment exists)

- ✔ **Clear Hyperlinks** and **Remove Hyperlinks:** Hyperlinks are not discussed in this book.

Filling a Series

Excel provides an AutoFill feature, which enables you to fill in several types of data series in a row or column. AutoFill uses the fill handle — the small square that appears at the bottom-right corner of the selected cell or range.

Excel provides an AutoFill Options Smart Tag next to the fill handle after you drag the fill handle to a new location. Click the AutoFill Options Smart Tag to display a list of commonly used fill options, such as Copy Cells, Fill Series, Fill Formatting Only, and Fill Without Formatting (see Figure 4-7).

Figure 4-7

Remember: If the selected cell or range doesn't have a fill handle, it means the AutoFill feature is turned off. To turn on the feature, follow these steps:

1. Click the File tab and then click the Options button.

2. In the Excel Options dialog box, click the Advanced category.

3. In the Editing options section, select the Enable Fill Handle and Cell Drag-and-Drop check box.

4. Click OK.

Remember: You can't use AutoFill if you make a multiple selection.

Entering a series of incremental values or dates

To use AutoFill to enter a series of incremental values, follow these steps:

1. Enter at least two values or dates in the series into adjacent cells. These values need not be consecutive.

2. Select the cells that you used in Step 1. (*See* "Selecting a range," later in this part, for details.)

3. Click and drag the fill handle to complete the series in the cells that you select. As you drag the fill handle, Excel displays a small box that tells you what it's planning to enter into each cell.

Remember: After you complete the drag operation, Excel displays the Auto Fill Options Smart Tag. You can click the Smart Tag to select a different fill option. For even more control, drag the fill handle while pressing the right mouse button. After you release the button, you see a list of options.

Remember: If one or more cells display a series of pound signs (such as ####) after you fill a number or date series, it means the column isn't wide enough to display the number or date. The solution is to make the column wider. *See* "Changing column width," in Part 8.

AutoFill works also in the negative direction. If you use AutoFill by starting with two cells that contain –20 and –19, for example, Excel fills in –18, –17, and so on.

If the values in the cells that you enter don't have equal increments, Excel completes the series by calculating a simple linear regression. This feature is handy for performing simple forecasts. *Note:* Excel calculates a simple linear regression or progression, depending on the direction (negative or positive) of the series.

Entering a series of text

Excel is familiar with some text series (days of the week, months of the year), and it can complete these series for you automatically.

Follow these steps to use AutoFill to complete a known series of text:

1. Enter any of the series into a cell (for example, **Monday** or **February**).

2. Click and drag the fill handle to complete the series in the cells that you select.

You can also teach Excel to recognize custom series that work with AutoFill. *See* "Sorting based on a custom sort order," in Part 13.

Inserting or Deleting Entire Rows and Columns

If you insert new rows or columns in Excel, the program places blank rows or columns in the worksheet, and surrounding rows or columns move out to accommodate the new rows or columns.

In certain circumstances, you may want to delete entire rows or columns from your worksheet. If you delete a row or rows, the rows below the deleted row(s) shift upward to fill the gap. If you delete a column or columns, the columns to the right of the deleted column(s) shift to the left to fill the gap.

Inserting entire rows and columns

To insert new rows or columns in your worksheet, follow these steps:

1. Select a cell *below* where you want to insert a row or to the *right* of where you want to insert a column. If you want to insert more than one row or column, select as many cells as rows or columns you're inserting (*See* "Selecting Cells and Ranges," later in this part.)

2. Choose one of the following options:

   • Right-click the selected cell(s) and choose Insert from the contextual menu.

- Press Ctrl+Shift++ (the plus sign on the top row of keys) or Ctrl++ (the plus sign on the numeric keypad).

After you choose an option, Excel displays the Insert dialog box.

3. Select either the Entire Row or Entire Column option button.

4. Click OK.

TIP ⊠ Insert ▾ In Step 2, you can click the arrow portion of the Insert split button on the Ribbon's Home tab and then choose Insert Sheet Rows or Insert Sheet Columns from the menu. Using this method eliminates Steps 3 and 4.

FAST TRACK You can quickly insert rows or columns by first clicking the row or column header where you want to insert the row or column, then right-clicking the selection, and then choosing Insert from the menu. *See* "Selecting entire rows and columns," later in this part.

Deleting entire rows and columns

To delete entire rows or columns, follow these steps:

1. Click the row header or column header of the row(s) or column(s) you want to delete. *See* "Selecting entire rows and columns," later in this part. Excel selects the row(s) or column(s).

2. With the mouse pointer on the selected row(s) or column(s), right-click and choose Delete from the menu.

Moving Cells and Ranges

Moving data in a cell or a range is common. You may, for example, need to relocate a range of data to make room for something else.

Moving data to a new location in the same worksheet

Follow these steps to move a cell or a range:

1. Select the cell or range to move. (*See* "Selecting Cells and Ranges," later in this part, for details.)

2. Click the Cut button on the Ribbon's Home tab. (You can also press Ctrl+X or right-click the cell or range and choose Cut from the contextual menu.)

3. Move the cell pointer to the range that will hold the copy (by clicking the cell or by navigating with the arrow keys). You need to select only the upper-left cell in the range.

4. Press Enter.

If the range that you're moving contains formulas that refer to other cells, the references continue to refer to the original cells. You almost always want references to continue to refer to the original cells.

If you decide that the location that you're moving to isn't too far away, you can follow these steps:

1. Select the cell or range to move. (***See*** "Selecting Cells and Ranges," later in this part.)

2. Move the mouse pointer to any of the selection's borders.

The mouse pointer changes to an arrow with a small directional cross at its tip.

3. Drag the mouse to the location where you want to move the cell or range.

4. Release the mouse button. Excel moves the cell or range to the new location.

If you press and hold Shift while dragging, Excel performs a move and an insert paste in a single operation, without the use of the Insert dialog box. The insert paste operation allows you to insert the cell or range inside another range.

Remember: If you change your mind after Step 2, press Esc to cancel the operation. If you change your mind after you move the data, you can click the undo button on the Quick Access toolbar or press Ctrl+Z.

Remember: If the mouse pointer doesn't change to an arrow in Step 2, your drag-and-drop feature is off. To turn on this feature, follow these steps:

1. Click the File tab, and then click the Options button.

2. In the Excel Options dialog box, click the Advanced tab.

3. In the Editing options section, select the Enable Fill Handle and Cell Drag-and-Drop check box.

4. To prevent accidental overwriting of data in the destination range, select the Alert before Overwriting Cells check box.

5. Click OK.

If you move data, make sure that you have enough blank cells to hold it. Except when you move data by dragging, Excel overwrites existing data without warning.

Moving data to a different worksheet or workbook

If you want to move the contents of a cell or range to a different worksheet or to a different workbook, follow these steps:

1. Select the cell or range to move. (***See*** "Selecting Cells and Ranges," later in this part, for details.)

 2. Click the Cut button on the Ribbon's Home tab. (You can also press Ctrl+X or right-click the cell or range and choose Cut from the contextual menu.)

3. Activate the worksheet you're moving to by clicking the sheet tab. If you're moving the selection to a sheet on a different workbook, activate that workbook first by clicking the Switch Windows button on the Ribbon's View tab and selecting the workbook from the menu. (You can select a different workbook also by selecting the workbook name on the Windows taskbar below the Excel window.) After you activate the workbook, select the destination worksheet for the data.

4. Move the cell pointer to the range that will hold the copy (by clicking the cell or by navigating with the arrow keys). You need to select only the upper-left cell in the range.

5. Press Enter.

 After you move data, make sure that you have enough blank cells to hold it. Excel overwrites existing data without warning.

 Remember: If you change your mind after Step 2, press Esc to cancel the operation. If you change your mind after you move the data, you can click the undo button on the Quick Access toolbar or press Ctrl+Z.

Replacing the Contents of a Cell

To replace the contents of a cell with something else, follow these steps:

1. Select the cell. (***See*** "Selecting a cell," later in this part, for details.)

2. Type your new entry. (It replaces the previous contents.)

Remember: Any formatting that you applied to the cell remains.

Searching for Data to Replace

Sometimes you may need to replace all occurrences of a value or text with something else. If your worksheet contains lots of data, you may find locating a particular piece of information difficult. A quick way to find something is to have Excel do it for you.

To replace all occurrences of a value or text with something else:

1. Click the Find & Select button on the Ribbon's Home tab and choose Replace from the menu. (Alternatively, press Ctrl+H.) Excel displays its Find and Replace dialog box with the Replace tab selected, as shown in Figure 4-8.

Figure 4-8

2. In the Find What drop-down list, enter the text or value to search for.

3. If you want to search for data with specific formatting:

    a. Click the Format button to the right of the Find What drop-down list. If the Format button isn't visible, click the Options button. Excel displays the Find Format dialog box.

    b. Select the appropriate tabs and, in each tab, specify the formatting that you're looking for.

    c. After you complete your selections, click OK to exit the Find Format dialog box.

TIP

If a cell in your worksheet already contains all the formatting you want to use in your search, click the arrow on the Format button to the right of the Find What drop-down list and select Choose Format From Cell. Excel adds an eyedropper icon to the cursor. Click the cell that has the formatting you require.

4. In the Replace With drop-down list, enter the text or value that should replace the text or value from Step 2.

5. If you want to specify new formatting for the replaced characters, click the Format button to the right of the Replace With drop-down list box and follow the procedure outlined in Step 3.

6. In the Within drop-down list box, select whether you want to look in the active sheet or the entire workbook for the information that you typed in Step 2. If the Within drop-down box isn't visible, click the Options button.

7. To have Excel search and replace all occurrences automatically, click the Replace All button. To verify each replacement instead, click the Find Next button. Excel pauses after it finds a match. To replace the found text, click Replace. To skip it and find the next match, click the Find Next button again. Click the Find All button to select a match from the drop-down window.

8. Click the Close button after you finish finding and replacing the text.

See also "Finding Specific Data," in Part 7.

Selecting Cells and Ranges

In Excel, you normally select a cell or range before performing an operation that works with the cell or range. Topics in this section describe how to make various types of cell and range selections.

Remember: Many dialog boxes in Excel provide a special text box called a *RefEdit* box, which allows you to enter or point to a range. When a dialog box includes a RefEdit box, you can choose to select the range in advance or after you display the dialog box. You encounter RefEdit boxes (although we may not explicitly refer to them as such) in various procedures we describe in this book.

Selecting a cell

To select a cell (and make it the active cell), use any of the following techniques:

  ✔ Use the arrow keys to move the cell pointer to the cell.

  ✔ Click the cell with the mouse pointer.

  ✔ Click the Find & Select button on the Ribbon's Home tab and choose Go To from the menu (or press F5 or Ctrl+G), enter the cell address in the Reference text box of the Go To dialog box that appears, and click OK.

The selected cell now has a dark border around it, and its address appears in the name box.

Selecting a range

You can select a range in any of the following ways:

  ✔ Click the mouse in a cell and drag to highlight the range. If you drag past the end of the screen, the worksheet scrolls.

  ✔ Move to the first cell of the range. Press F8, and then move the cell pointer with the direction keys to highlight the range. Press F8 again to return the arrow keys to normal movement.

✔ Press Shift as you use the arrow keys to select a range.

✔ Click the Find & Select button on the Ribbon's Home tab and choose Go To from the menu (or press F5 or Ctrl+G), enter a range's address in the Reference text box of the Go To dialog box that appears, and click OK.

Selecting noncontiguous ranges

Most of the time, the ranges that you select are *contiguous* — they are a single rectangle of cells. Excel also enables you to work with noncontiguous ranges, which consist of two or more ranges (or single cells) that aren't necessarily next to each other (also known as a *multiple selection*).

To apply the same formatting to cells in different areas of your worksheet, for example, one approach is to make a multiple selection. After you select the appropriate cells or ranges, Excel applies the formatting that you choose to all the selected cells. Figure 4-9 shows two noncontiguous ranges (B2:G2 and B6:G6) that have been selected.

Figure 4-9

	B6	▼ (	*fx*	488				
	A	B	C	D	E	F	G	H
1		January	February	March	April	May	June	
2	Celery	442	222	112	324	448	464	
3	Cauliflower	447	69	62	284	343	196	
4	Okra	292	440	252	378	277	311	
5	Mushroom	366	85	453	392	364	92	
6	Artichoke	488	480	173	478	65	176	
7	Broccoli	308	80	109	472	206	339	
8								
9								

You can select a noncontiguous range in any of the following ways:

✔ Drag the mouse to select the first range, then press and hold Ctrl as you drag the mouse to select the other ranges.

✔ From the keyboard, select the first range by pressing F8 and then using the arrow keys. After selecting the first range, press Shift+F8, move the cell pointer using the arrow keys, and press F8 to start selecting another range.

✔ Click the Find & Select button on the Ribbon's Home tab, choose Go To from the menu (or press F5 or Ctrl+G), and enter a range's address in the Reference text box of the Go To dialog box that appears. Separate the different ranges with a comma. Click OK, and Excel selects the cells in the ranges that you specify.

Selecting entire rows and columns

You can select entire rows or columns in any of the following ways:

✔ Click the row or column heading to select a single row or column.

✔ To select multiple adjacent rows or columns, click a row or column heading and drag to highlight additional rows or columns.

✔ To select multiple (nonadjacent) rows or columns, press Ctrl as you click the row or column headings that you want.

✔ Press Ctrl+spacebar to select the column of the active cell or the columns of the selected range.

✔ Press Shift+spacebar to select the row of the active cell or the rows of the selected cells.

✔ Click the Select All button at the intersection of the row and column headers, or press Ctrl+A or Ctrl+Shift+spacebar to select all cells in the worksheet. Selecting all cells is the same as selecting all columns and all rows.

Selecting a multisheet (3-D) range

An Excel workbook can contain more than one worksheet, and a range can extend across multiple worksheets. You can think of these as three-dimensional ranges.

To select a multisheet range, follow these steps:

1. Select a cell or range on the active sheet. *See* "Selecting a range," earlier in this part.

2. Group the sheets that will be in the range. *See* "Grouping and Ungrouping Worksheets," in Part 3.

After you select a multisheet range, you can perform the same operations that you can perform on a single sheet range. Any changes that you make to one sheet (formatting, entering or editing data, and so on) are reflected in the other sheets.

Transposing a Range

If you need to change the orientation of a range, Excel can do it for you in a snap. After you transpose a range, the data that was in rows is transferred to columns and vice versa. Figure 4-10 shows an example of a horizontal range that we transposed to a vertical range.

Figure 4-10

		C	D	E	F	G	H
		Jan	Feb	Mar	Apr	May	Jun
		3129	6684	5991	2849	5938	2600
		Jan	3129				
		Feb	6684				
		Mar	5991				
8		Apr	2849				
9		May	5938				
10		Jun	2600				
11							

The transpose operation is nothing more than a special paste option. To transpose a range, therefore, follow the steps outlined in "Copying a range to another range," earlier in this part, but in Step 4, select the Transpose option from the Paste Options gallery. Ensure that the transposed range doesn't overlap the nontransposed range.

After you transpose a range, delete the original range if required.

Remember: Excel adjusts any formulas in the original range so that they work correctly after you transpose them.

Undoing Changes and Mistakes

One very useful feature in Excel is its multilevel Undo feature. This feature enables you to reverse your recent actions, one step at a time. If you discover that you accidentally deleted a range of data several minutes ago, for example, you can use the Undo feature to successively undo your actions until the deleted range reappears.

To undo an operation, use any of the following techniques:

- ✔ Click the undo button on the Quick Access toolbar until you arrive at the action that you want to undo.

- ✔ Press Ctrl+Z until you arrive at the action that you want to undo.

- ✔ Click the arrow on the undo button on the Quick Access toolbar. This action displays a description of your recent actions. Select the actions that you want to undo.

In Excel 2007 and Excel 2010, you can undo a maximum of 100 operations. In earlier versions of Excel, you can undo only a maximum of 16 operations.

Validating Data Entry

You can specify the type of data that a cell can accept. If you develop a spreadsheet that others use, for example, you can limit the range of values that a user may enter into input cells. Excel then validates the input to ensure that the values the user enters fall within the range you specified. Excel displays an error message if a user enters an invalid value.

To specify data-entry validation criteria, follow these steps:

1. Select the cell or range that you want to validate. (*See* "Selecting Cells and Ranges," earlier in this part, for details.)

2. Click the Data tab on the Ribbon and click the upper portion of the Data Validation split button (the portion with the icon) or click the arrow on the button and choose Data Validation from the menu. Excel displays the Data Validation dialog box.

3. Click the Settings tab, and specify the type of data that the cell should have by selecting an entry from the Allow drop-down list box and the Data drop-down list box, if applicable.

You can specify any of the following options to validate data entered in a cell:

- Whole numbers within specified limits.

- Decimal numbers within specified limits.

- A list of predefined choices. You can enter the list choices directly into the list Source box (separating each choice with a comma), or you can use a range reference, which stores the choices in individual cells in the range. After you specify the list, a drop-down arrow appears in a validation cell when you select it.

- Dates within specified limits.

- Times within specified limits.

- The length of entered text or numbers within specified limits. Note that Excel refers to this option as Text Length, although it's applicable to both the length of a text string and the number of digits in a number (or a combination of text and numbers).

- A Custom validation. You can enter a Boolean formula (a formula that returns a True or a False value) to specify a validation rule. If the formula returns False, the validation rule is invoked. For example, if you specify a data validation entry range in a column that starts at cell A2, the formula =A2>A1 ensures that each value entered in the range is greater than the value above it. (Excel automatically adjusts the validation reference for each cell in the range, so for cell A3 the formula is =A3>A2, and so on.)

4. To specify a message to appear after a user clicks an input cell, click the Input Message tab and type a message in the Input Message text box. If you want a title to appear at the top of the message, enter a title in the Title text box.

5. To specify a custom error message to appear in a dialog box if someone enters invalid data, click the Error Alert tab and type a message in the Error Message text box. If you want a title to appear at the top of the message, enter a title in the Title text box.

   Choose a style for the error message from the Style drop-down list box (Stop, Warning, or Information). Each style that you select displays an error icon and various buttons on the error dialog box as follows:

   - Stop: Displays Retry and Cancel buttons.

   - Warning: Displays Yes, No, and Cancel buttons. (Clicking Yes enters the invalid data.)

   - Information: Displays OK and Cancel buttons. (Clicking OK enters the invalid data.)

6. Click OK.

If you subsequently want to remove the validation criteria from a cell or range, select the cell or range, click the upper portion of the Data Validation split button on the Ribbon's Data tab, and click the Clear All button in the Data Validation dialog box that appears.

Remember: If you don't specify a message in Step 5, Excel uses a default message if a data-entry error occurs.

You can combine data validation with worksheet protection to permit only validated input cells to be altered. ***See*** "Protecting a Worksheet," in Part 3.

Using Formulas and Functions

This part deals with topics related to formulas and functions. Formulas make using spreadsheets valuable by allowing you to calculate results from data stored in the worksheet. Functions are built-in or custom tools used in formulas. They can make your formulas perform powerful feats and save you a great deal of time.

In this part . . .

- ✔ Using Absolute, Relative, and Mixed References
- ✔ Converting Formulas to Values
- ✔ Entering Functions in Formulas
- ✔ Referencing Cells or Ranges in Other Worksheets or Workbooks

Absolute, Relative, and Mixed References

If you copy a formula containing an *absolute reference,* Excel doesn't adjust the reference in the copied cell. (An absolute reference uses two dollar signs in its address, one for the column part and one for the row part.) On the other hand, Excel adjusts *relative references* as you copy the formula.

Excel also enables you to use *mixed references,* in which only one part of the address is absolute. The following table summarizes all possible types of cell references and shows how a reference changes after it is copied one cell down or one cell across. In all cases, the absolute portion of the reference is unchanged.

Type	Example	Down	Across
Relative reference	=A1	=A2	=B1
Absolute reference	=$A$1	=$A$1	=$A$1
Mixed reference (column part is absolute)	=$A1	=$A2	=$A1
Mixed reference (row part is absolute)	=A$1	=A$1	=B$1

To change the type of cell reference in a formula, follow these steps:

1. Double-click the cell containing the formula (or press F2) to get into edit mode.

2. In the cell or formula bar, click the mouse pointer on the cell reference.

3. Press F4 repeatedly to cycle through all possible cell reference types. Stop after the cell reference displays the type you want to use.

4. Press Enter to complete the operation.

Basic Formula Essentials

Every Excel formula begins with an equal sign. A formula can consist of up to 8,192 characters and include any of the following elements:

- Operators such as + (for addition) and * (for multiplication)
- Absolute, relative, or mixed cell references, such as $A$1 or B2:G10
- Named references, such as Revenue or Profit
- Values, text, or logical values
- Worksheet functions (such as SUM or AVERAGE)

Note that in versions prior to Excel 2007, a formula can consist of no more than 1,024 characters.

After you enter a formula into a cell, the cell displays the result of the formula. You see the formula itself in the *formula bar* as the cell activates. (The formula bar lies below the Ribbon.)

Operator precedence is the set of rules that Excel uses to perform its calculations in a formula.

The following table provides the list of operators that you can use in formulas and indicates each operator's precedence.

Operator	Name	Precedence
^	Exponentiation (raised to a power)	1
*	Multiplication	2
/	Division	2
+	Addition	3
−	Subtraction	3
&	Concatenation (joins text)	4
=	Equal to	5
>	Greater than	5
<	Less than	5

The table shows that exponentiation has the highest precedence (that is, Excel performs it first), and logical comparisons have the lowest precedence. If two operators have the same precedence, Excel performs the calculations from left to right.

Remember: You can override operator precedence by using parentheses in your formulas. In the formula = (Income-Expenses) *TaxRate, for example, Expenses are subtracted from Income, and the result is multiplied by TaxRate.

Changing When Formulas Are Calculated

If the Excel calculation mode is set to automatic (the default), changing cells that you use in a formula causes the formula to display a new result automatically.

To set the Excel calculation mode to manual, click the Formulas tab on the Ribbon, click the Options button in the Calculation group, and choose Manual from the menu.

Remember: If you're working in manual calculation mode, Excel displays Calculate in the status bar if you have any uncalculated formulas. Do one of the following to recalculate the formulas:

✔ Click the Formulas tab on the Ribbon and click the Calculate Now button in the Calculation group or press F9. The formulas in all open workbooks are immediately calculated.

✔ Click the Formulas tab on the Ribbon and click the Calculate Sheet button in the Calculation group or press Shift+F9. The formulas in the active worksheet only are immediately calculated. Other worksheets in the same workbook aren't calculated.

Remember: The Excel calculation mode isn't specific to a particular worksheet. If you change the calculation mode, that change affects all open workbooks and not just the active workbook.

To return to automatic calculation mode, click the Formulas tab on the Ribbon, click the Options button in the Calculation group, and choose Automatic from the menu.

Converting Formulas to Values

Sometimes, you may want to convert a formula to its current value (remove the formula and leave only its result). For example, you may want to prevent future changes to the value of a cell if other cells that the formula references change.

To convert a formula to its current value, follow these steps:

1. Select the cell that contains the formula. To convert several formulas, you can select a range.

2. Click the Copy button on the Ribbon's Home tab. (You can also press Ctrl+C or right-click the cell and choose Copy from the contextual menu.)

3. Click the arrow portion of the Paste button on the Ribbon's Home tab and choose an option in the Paste Values section of the Paste Options gallery.

4. Press Enter or Esc to exit Copy mode.

Remember: This procedure overwrites the formulas. To put the current values of the formulas in a different (empty) area of the worksheet, select a new cell or the upper-left cell of a new range before Step 3.

Editing Functions in Formulas

After you create a formula with one or more functions, you may want to modify the arguments in one of the functions later. Excel provides several ways for you to modify a function. The method you choose depends on personal choice and the complexity of the function.

Use any of the following techniques to modify a function:

✔ If your formula contains only one function or if the function you want to modify is the last one in the formula, click the Insert Function button on the formula bar (or on the Formulas tab of the Ribbon), or press Shift+F3 to display the Insert Function dialog box for the function.

✔ If your formula contains more than one function, press F2 or double-click the formula cell. Position the cursor within the function that you want to modify and click the Insert Function button, or press Shift+F3.

✔ The most efficient way to modify simple functions (that is, those with few arguments) is to do so manually. Excel provides a ScreenTip (floating text) for the function to help you identify the names and order of the function's arguments.

See also "Entering Functions in Formulas," immediately following this section.

Entering Functions in Formulas

Excel provides more than 300 built-in functions that can make your formulas perform powerful feats and save you a great deal of time. Functions perform the following tasks:

✔ Simplify your formulas

✔ Enable formulas to perform calculations that are otherwise impossible

✔ Enable conditional execution of formulas — giving them some rudimentary decision-making capability

Most worksheet functions use one or more arguments, enclosed in parentheses. Think of an argument as a piece of information that clarifies what you want the function to do. For example, the following function (which rounds the number in cell A1 to two decimal places) uses two arguments:

`=ROUND(A1,2)`

Remember: You can *nest* a function within another function. The formula `=SUM(MAX(B1:B6),ROUND(A1,2))`, for example, nests the MAX and ROUND functions in the SUM function. This example sums the maximum value in the range B1 to B6 and the value in cell A1, rounded to two decimal places.

See also "Editing Functions in Formulas," immediately preceding this section.

Entering functions manually

Even if you're not familiar with the function that you want to use, you can begin typing the function name and Excel's Formula AutoComplete feature will drop down a list of possible matches, as shown in Figure 5-1.

Figure 5-1

If you continue typing without selecting a name from the list, Excel narrows the available choices. If you want to select a function name from the list, you can either double-click with the mouse or highlight the name (using the mouse or arrow keys) and press the Tab key. Excel inserts the function in the formula and includes an opening parenthesis.

Excel provides assistance for the functions in the drop-down list in the form of ScreenTips (see Figure 5-1). Each ScreenTip provides a brief description of the function's use.

Excel provides you with further assistance after you type the entire function name manually (including the opening parenthesis) or you select the function from the drop-down list. This assistance enables you to determine the number and order of arguments in the function. Excel displays a ScreenTip below the function you're typing. The ScreenTip includes the name of the function you typed followed by the names of all the function's mandatory and optional arguments in parentheses. To display a Help window for the function, click the function name in the ScreenTip.

See also "Entering formulas manually," in Part 4.

Using the AutoSum tool

The AutoSum tool provides a quick method for you to enter commonly used functions.

To use the AutoSum tool, follow these steps:

1. Click a cell below or to the right of a range of numbers you want to aggregate.

Σ ▾ 2. Perform one of the following actions:

- To sum the range, click the AutoSum button on the Ribbon's Home tab or Formulas tab. Excel places a *marquee* (also known as *marching ants*) around cells that it thinks you want to sum. If the range of cells that the marquee surrounds isn't the range that you want to sum, use the mouse to highlight a new range. Click the AutoSum button again or press Enter to complete the operation.

- To find the average, count, minimum, or maximum of the range, click the arrow on the AutoSum button to display a menu for selecting these operations. Click the operation that you want to perform from the menu, and follow the procedure that we describe for summing the range after Excel places the marquee around the cells.

 TIP Excel automatically places a marquee around the first region that it encounters above or to the left of the formula cell. A *region* is a range that contains nonblank cells. To select multiple regions as you use the AutoSum tool in Step 2, press and hold Ctrl while dragging the mouse over each region. *See also* "Selecting Cells and Ranges," in Part 4.

Using the Function Library

The Function Library enables you to easily enter a function and its arguments. The Function Library is particularly useful if you're not sure of the function you're looking for and want to browse through the available choices. To make it easier to find what you're looking for, Excel groups the available functions into well-known categories, such as financial and text.

To enter a function by using the Function Library, follow these steps:

1. Activate the cell that will contain the function. If you're inserting the function into an existing formula, click the formula at the position where you want to insert the function.

2. If you're inserting a new function adjacent to another function in a formula, you must add an operator (for example, +, –, or *) or a comma at this point to delimit the two functions.

3. Click the Formulas tab on the Ribbon and click a function category in the Function Library group. You can click the More Functions button if the category you want is not shown in the Functions Library group.

4. Choose a function that you want from the menu. Excel displays the Function Arguments dialog box, as shown in Figure 5-2. The Function Arguments dialog box prompts you for each argument of the function that you select. You can enter the arguments manually, or you can point to them in the worksheet if they're cell references. The Function Arguments dialog box displays the result.

To get help with the function, click Help on This Function in the Function Arguments dialog box. Excel displays the Help window for the function.

5. After you specify all the required arguments, click OK.

Figure 5-2

Modifying a Range Reference Used in a Function

If you edit a cell that contains a formula, Excel color-codes the references in the formula and places an outline around each cell or range that the formula references. The color of the outline corresponds to the color that appears in the formula. Each outlined cell or range also contains *fill handles* (a small square in each corner of the outlined cell or range). See Figure 5-3.

Figure 5-3

Fill handles   Outline in color

If your formula contains a function that uses a range argument, you can easily modify the range reference by following these steps:

1. To begin editing the formula, press F2 or double-click the cell. **See also** "Editing the Contents of a Cell," in Part 4.

2. Locate the range that the function uses. (The range appears with an outline.)

3. Drag a fill handle to extend or contract the range. You can also click a border of the outlined range and move the outline to a new range. In either case, Excel changes the range reference in the formula.

4. Press Enter.

Remember: Formulas that contain name references place a colored outline around the named cell or range. The outline doesn't provide fill handles, however, or enable you to move this type of reference by clicking a border of the outline.

Referencing Cells or Ranges in Other Workbooks

External references to other workbooks are also known as *links*. The workbook that contains the link formulas (external reference formulas) is the *destination* workbook. The workbook that is the source of the data that the external reference formula uses is the *source* workbook. Note that the source workbook doesn't need to remain open while you are working in the destination workbook.

Referencing cells in other workbooks

If your formula needs to refer to a cell in a different workbook, use the following format for your formula:

```
=[WorkbookName]SheetName!CellAddress
```

The workbook name (in brackets), the worksheet name, and an exclamation point precede the cell address. Such a formula is sometimes known as a *link formula* or an *external reference*.

Remember: If either the workbook name or the worksheet name in the reference includes one or more spaces, you must enclose it (and the sheet name) in single quotation marks. The following formula, for example, refers to a cell on Sheet1 in a workbook named Budget For 2005:

```
=A1*'[Budget For 2005]Sheet1'!A1
```

If a formula refers to cells in a different workbook, the other workbook doesn't need to remain open. If the workbook is closed, you must add the complete path to the reference. For example:

```
=A1* 'C:\My Documents\Excel\[Budget For 2005]Sheet1'!A1
```

TIP The easiest way to enter formulas that require external links is by pointing. You must have all source workbooks open. *See* "Arranging Windows Automatically," in Part 2 and "Entering formulas by pointing," in Part 4.

To avoid problems that can occur in formulas in the destination workbook when you insert or delete rows, columns, or cells or otherwise move linked cells or ranges in source workbooks, we strongly recommend that you use names for cells or ranges that the dependent workbook references in the source workbooks.

Managing links

As you work with external references in a worksheet, occasionally you may need to perform a few management tasks. Excel provides the Edit Links dialog box to help you with these tasks.

To display the Edit Links dialog box (see Figure 5-4), click the Edit Links button on the Ribbon's Data tab. The button is disabled if your workbook contains no links (external references) to another workbook.

Figure 5-4

The window in the Edit Links dialog box lists all the source workbooks that your destination workbook is connected to. You can perform the following operations in the Edit Links dialog box:

- ✔ **Update Values:** If you need to update the values from external workbooks during your working session, you can do so by using this button.

  Select the source workbook or workbooks in the window and click Update Values.

- ✔ **Change Source:** If the location or name of a source workbook changes, you have to update the link information.

  In the window, select the source workbook whose name has changed and click Change Source. In the Change Source dialog box, navigate to the location of the new source file, select the file, and click OK.

- ✔ **Open Source:** The Edit Links dialog box provides a convenient location from which to open source workbooks.

  In the window, select the workbook(s) you want to open and click Open Source. Excel opens all the workbooks that you select.

✔ **Break Link:** If you want to retain the current values (not formulas) from one or more source workbooks, and you no longer want to link to the source(s), you can break the links to the source workbook(s).

In the window, select the workbook(s) with which you want to sever the links and click Break Link. Because you cannot undo the operation, Excel prompts you for confirmation. Click Break Links in the confirmation message box to permanently break the links.

✔ **Check Status:** Whenever you open the Edit Links dialog box, the Status column in the window displays as Unknown. Excel doesn't automatically display the current status of links.

Click the Check Status button to see the current status of links. A status of OK, Source is open, or Value updated from <*filename*> indicates that no action is required on the user's part. However, if the status displays a warning or error message for a source workbook, the user must update the values, change the source, or open the source. The specific error or warning message indicates the required action.

✔ **[Change] Startup Prompt:** By default, when you open a workbook containing external references (the destination workbook), Excel prompts you to update links if any source workbooks are not already open. (Links are updated automatically when source workbooks are open.) However, you can control the prompting and updating behavior when opening a workbook.

Click the Startup Prompt button. Excel displays a dialog box with the following three choices:

- *Let users choose to display the alert or not.* After selecting this option, the user must then turn the alert display on or off as follows: Click the File tab and then click the Options button. In the Excel Options dialog box, click the Advanced category and scroll down to the General section. Finally, select or deselect the Ask to Update Automatic Links check box.

  If you deselect the check box, Excel automatically updates the links without displaying a prompt when you open a dependent workbook. Note that this option affects the *current* user only and applies to every dependent workbook that the current user opens. The option does not affect any other user with whom you share the workbook.

- *Don't display the alert and don't update automatic links.* This option is self-explanatory and affects all users with whom you share the workbook.

- *Don't display the alert and update links.* This option is self-explanatory, and affects all users with whom you share the workbook.

Referencing Cells or Ranges in Other Worksheets

If your formula needs to refer to a cell in a different worksheet in the same workbook, use the following format for your formula:

```
SheetName!CellAddress
```

Precede the cell address with the worksheet name, and follow it with an exclamation point.

Remember: If the worksheet name in the reference includes one or more spaces, you must enclose the name in single quotation marks. The following is a formula that refers to a cell on a sheet by the name of All Depts:

```
=A1*'All Depts'!A1
```

An easy way to enter a range reference on another worksheet is by pointing with the mouse. **See** "Entering formulas by pointing," in Part 4.

If you need to reference a 3-D range in a function, enter the range in the following format:

```
=FunctionName(FirstSheet:LastSheet!RangeReference)
```

For example:

```
=SUM(Sheet2:Sheet4!$A$1:$A$10)
```

The following rules apply to 3-D range references:

- ✔ The range includes all sheets between the first and last sheet names in the reference, inclusive.

- ✔ If you insert another sheet between the first and last sheets, it will be included in the reference automatically.

- ✔ You can use absolute or relative references in the range reference.

- ✔ You can use any valid names for the sheets, but if any name has a space, you must use single quotes to enclose the names in the reference. For example:

  ```
  =SUM('Dept Engineering:Dept HR'!$A$1:$A$10)
  ```

Remember: Less than 10 percent of Excel's functions support 3-D range references and those that do fall mostly in the statistical category.

You can point with the mouse to create a 3-D reference. First position the mouse pointer in the function where the reference will be placed. Then select the cell or range in the first worksheet that will be included in the reference. Next, press and hold Shift and click the sheet tab of the last sheet in the reference. Press Enter to complete the procedure.

Creating and Using Names

Dealing with cryptic cell and range addresses can be confusing. Fortunately, Excel enables you to assign descriptive names to cells and ranges. For example, you can name a cell `InterestRate` or name a range `JulySales`.

In this part . . .

- ✔ **Applying Names to Existing Cell References**
- ✔ **Creating, Deleting, and Editing Names**
- ✔ **Managing Names**
- ✔ **Naming Constants and Formulas**
- ✔ **Pasting Names into a Formula**

Advantages to Naming Cells and Ranges

Using names for cells and ranges offers the following advantages:

✔ A meaningful range name (such as Income) is much easier to remember than a range address (such as A1: A21).

✔ After you select a named cell or range, its name appears in the name box.

✔ You can quickly move to a named area of your worksheet by choosing a name in the name box.

✔ Creating formulas is easier because you can paste a cell or range name into a formula.

✔ Names make your formulas more understandable and easier to use. For example, =Income-Taxes is more intuitive than =D20-D40.

Although Excel is flexible about the names that you can define, it does have the following rules:

✔ Names must begin with a letter or the underscore character (_).

✔ Names can't contain any spaces. You may want to use an underscore or a period character to simulate a space (such as Annual_Total or Annual. Total).

✔ You can use any combination of letters and numbers, but the name must not begin with a number (such as 3rdQuarter) or look like a cell reference (such as Q3).

✔ You can't use most symbols. You can, however, use the underscore (_), period (.), backslash (\), and question mark (?).

✔ Names can be no more than 255 characters long.

Excel also reserves a few names internally for its own use. Avoid using the following for names: Print_Area, Print_Titles, Consolidate_Area, and Sheet_Title.

Applying Names to Existing Cell References

If you create a new name for a cell or a range, Excel doesn't automatically use the name in place of existing references in your formulas. For example, if you have a formula such as =A1*20 and then give a name to cell A1, the formula continues to display A1 (not the new name). Replacing cell or range references with their corresponding names, however, is fairly easy.

To apply names to cell references in existing formulas, follow these steps:

1. Select the range with the formulas that you want to modify.

2. Click the Formulas tab on the Ribbon, click the arrow on the Define Name button, and choose Apply Names from the menu. Excel displays the Apply Names dialog box, as shown in Figure 6-1.

Figure 6-1

3. Select the names that you want to apply by clicking them in turn.

4. Click OK. Excel replaces the range references with the names in the selected cells.

TIP

If you select a nonformula cell in Step 1, Excel applies the names to all applicable formulas in the worksheet.

Creating Names

Excel provides several useful methods for creating names. The method you choose depends on personal preference and techniques that may allow you to save time.

Creating a name using the New Name dialog box

To create a range name using the New Name dialog box, follow these steps:

1. Select the cell or range that you want to name.

2. Click the Formulas tab on the Ribbon and then click the Define Name button (or right-click the range and choose Name a Range from the contextual menu). Excel displays the New Name dialog box, as shown in Figure 6-2.

Figure 6-2

3. In the Name text box, type a name (or use the name that Excel proposes, if any).

4. If needed, enter a comment in the Comment box. You can enter a comment, for example, to provide a description and other details of the name for future worksheet auditing purposes.

5. Verify that the address Excel displays in the Refers To text box is correct. To refer to a different address, delete the address and then either type the new cell or range address (with a leading equal sign) or use the mouse pointer to select the cell or range on the worksheet.

6. Click OK.

If you want to create several names in one go, use the Name Manager instead of the Define Name method. Click the Name Manager button in the Formulas tab. In the Name Manager dialog box, click New to add a name. After you finish adding a name, you're returned to the Name Manager dialog box, where you can repeat the process to create additional names.

Creating a name using the name box

The name box is on the left side of the formula bar, as shown in Figure 6-3.

Name box   Name box divider

Figure 6-3

Resize cursor

To create a name by using the name box, follow these steps:

1. Select the cell or range to name.

2. Click the name box, and enter the name.

3. Press Enter to create the name.

Remember: If a name already exists, you can't use the name box to change the reference for the name. Attempting to do so simply displays the already existing name.

You can increase the width of the name box so that you can see more of longer names. Drag the name box divider (the area around the dimple in Figure 6-3) to the left or right.

Creating names from row and column labels

Your worksheet may contain column or row labels that you want to use for naming adjacent cells or ranges. Figure 6-4 shows a range of data with month labels in the left column and regions on the top row. You can create a name for each row in the range using the labels in the left column or create a name for each column in the range using the labels in the top row. You can also use both the top row and the left column to name simultaneously each row and each column in the range.

Figure 6-4

To create names by using adjacent row or column labels, follow these steps:

1. Select the name labels and the cells that you want to name. The labels must be adjacent to the cells that you're naming. A multiple selection isn't possible here.

2. Click the Formulas tab on the Ribbon and then click the Create from Selection button. The Create Names from Selection dialog box appears. Excel guesses how to create the names by checking the appropriate Create Names From Values In The check boxes. If the labels are on the left of the cells that you want to name, for example, Excel selects the Left Column option.

3. If Excel's selection isn't what you want, clear the selection and select the correct Create Names From Values In The check boxes as necessary.

4. Click OK to create the names.

If you create names from both row and column labels, you can refer to an entry in your table by the intersection of the row and column labels. In Figure 6-4, for example, I created names from the top row and left column labels in the range. You can create a formula like this: =A1*Mar North, where Mar North = 3575.

Remember: If the label that a cell contains results in an invalid name, Excel modifies the name to make it valid. If Excel encounters a value or a formula where a text label should be, however, it doesn't convert it to a valid name. It simply doesn't create a name.

Remember: The names that you create do *not* include the cells with the labels.

Creating sheet-level names

Normally, you can use a name that you create anywhere within the workbook. Names, by default, are book-level rather than sheet-level in *scope*. But what if you have several worksheets in a workbook and you want to use the same name (such as Dept_Total) in each sheet to signify different values? You need to create sheet-level names.

To define a sheet-level name, follow these steps:

1. Complete Steps 1–5 in the procedure for "Creating a name using the New Name dialog box," earlier in this part.

2. Click the Scope drop-down list and select the sheet name to which the name you're defining will belong. Although you can select any sheet name from the list, you'll normally want to choose the sheet with your selected cell or range.

3. Click OK.

You also can create a sheet-level name by using the name box. Select the cell or range, click the name box, and enter the name, preceding it with the sheet's name (surrounded with single quotes if the name contains spaces) and an exclamation point. For example, if you want to create a sheet-level name of Dept_Total in a sheet named Human Resources, enter 'Human Resources'!Dept_Total in the name box.

Remember: If you write a formula that uses a sheet-level name in the sheet where you define it, you don't need to include the worksheet name in the range name. (The name box doesn't display the worksheet name either.) If you use the name in a formula on a different worksheet, however, you must use the entire name (sheet name, exclamation point, and name).

Creating multisheet names

Names can extend into the third dimension — across multiple worksheets in a workbook. Multisheet names must include contiguous worksheets and must refer to the same cell or range reference in each worksheet. To create a multisheet name, follow these steps:

1. Click the Formulas tab on the Ribbon and then click the Define Name button. Excel displays the New Name dialog box.

2. In the Name text box, type a name (or use the name that Excel proposes, if any).

3. In the Refers To text box, enter the reference (and remember to begin it with an equal sign). The format for a multisheet reference is

   `FirstSheet:LastSheet!RangeReference`

4. Click OK.

An easier way to enter the reference in Step 3 is by pointing. Follow these steps after Step 2 (of the preceding list) to create a multisheet reference by pointing:

1. Click the tab of the first worksheet in the range, if it isn't already selected.

2. Click the Refers To text box, and delete the suggested reference (which usually isn't the one you want).

3. Press and hold Shift, and click the tab of the last worksheet that you want to include in the reference.

4. Select the cell or range in the first worksheet that you want to include in the name reference. The Refers To text box displays the multisheet range.

5. Click OK.

Deleting Names

If you no longer need a defined name, you can delete it by following these steps:

1. Click the Formulas tab on the Ribbon and then click the Name Manager button. Excel displays the Name Manager dialog box.

2. In the list, select the name that you want to delete and then click the Delete button. Excel asks you to confirm the deletion.

3. Click OK to delete.

If you change your mind after deleting the name, Excel allows you to undo the deletion. Click the undo button on the Quick Access toolbar or press Ctrl+Z. Earlier versions of Excel don't allow you to undo a name deletion.

4. Select another name to delete or click Close to exit the Name Manager dialog box.

 Be careful when deleting names. If you use the name in a formula, deleting the name causes the formula to become invalid. (Excel displays #NAME?.)

 If you delete the rows or columns that contain named cells or ranges, the names contain an invalid reference. For example, if cell A1 on Sheet1 is named Interest and you delete row 1 or column A, Interest then refers to =Sheet1!#REF! (that is, an erroneous reference). If you use the name Interest in a formula, the formula displays #REF.

Editing Names

Editing names is simple with the Name Manager. You can modify the name, scope, comment, or reference. Follow these steps to edit a name in the workbook:

1. Click the Formulas tab on the Ribbon and then click the Name Manager button. Excel displays the Name Manager dialog box.

2. In the list, select the name you want to change and then click the Edit button. Excel displays the Edit Name dialog box.

3. Enter a new name, comment, reference, or scope for the name and then click OK.

4. Select another name to edit or click Close to exit the dialog box.

Managing Names

It's not unusual for a workbook to contain dozens, hundreds, or even thousands of defined names. This situation makes tasks such as deleting multiple names, renaming names, and finding broken names challenging. Excel provides a Name Manager dialog box that you can use to view and manage the defined names in a workbook, as shown in Figure 6-5. To display the Name Manager dialog box, click the Formulas tab on the Ribbon and then click the Name Manager button.

Figure 6-5

Using the Name Manager dialog, you can

- ✔ View information for existing defined names, such as name, value, scope, reference, and comment. **See also** "Creating sheet-level names," earlier in this part, for a discussion of a name's scope.

- ✔ Create new names by clicking the New button to display the New Name dialog box.

- ✔ Edit existing names by selecting the name and clicking the Edit button to display the Edit Name dialog box.

- ✔ Delete multiple names at once by selecting the names (hold down Shift or Ctrl to select the names) and clicking the Delete button.

- ✔ Sort any column by clicking the column header.

- ✔ Resize the dialog box so that you can see more information. Dragging the top or bottom side outward allows you to see more names. Dragging the right or left side outward allows you to see more information in the name window and longer references in the Refers To box.

- ✔ Filter the list of names based on common criteria by clicking the Filter button and selecting an option from the menu. The menu is separated into three filter categories and you can select (through successive mouse clicks) an option in each category.

Naming Constants and Formulas

Names that you use in Excel don't need to refer to a cell or a range. You can give a name to a constant or even to a formula. If formulas in your worksheet refer to an interest rate (such as .085, or 8.5 percent), for example, you can define a name for this particular constant and then use it in your formulas. Alternatively, you can create a name that refers to a formula such as =SUM($A$1:$A$10) and use the name in your worksheet formulas.

To define a name for a constant or formula, follow these steps:

1. Click the Formulas tab on the Ribbon and then click the Define Name button. Excel displays the New Name dialog box.

2. In the Name text box, type a name for the constant or formula.

3. If needed, enter a comment in the Comment box. You can enter a comment, for example, to provide a description of the name for future worksheet auditing purposes.

4. In the Refers To text box, enter the value for the constant or the expression for the formula. Normally, this field holds a cell or range reference, but you can also enter a value or formula.

5. Click OK.

After performing these steps, you can use the name in your formulas.

Pasting Names into a Formula

If your formula uses named cells or ranges, you can type the name in place of the address. Another approach is to select the name from a list and have Excel insert the name for you automatically at your cursor location in the formula. You can do so in two ways:

✔ Click the Formulas tab on the Ribbon, click the Use in Formula button, and then select a name from the list.

✔ Press F3 to display the Paste Name dialog box, select a name from the list, and click OK.

Auditing Your Work

When your worksheets begin to get larger and more complex, ensuring accuracy becomes more difficult. That's why, for all but the most basic spreadsheets, auditing is an important task. *Auditing* refers to the process of tracking down and identifying errors in your worksheet. Excel provides a set of interactive auditing tools as well as other tools that are useful in the auditing process (although these other tools are not dedicated to this purpose).

In this part . . .

- Checking for Specific Worksheet Errors
- Evaluating Parts of a Formula
- Tracing Cell Relationships
- Understanding Formula Error Values
- Using the Watch Window

Checking for Specific Worksheet Errors

Excel can alert you regarding specific types of errors or potential errors in your worksheet. Excel can flag the following types of errors:

- ✔ Formulas that evaluate to error values (for example, #DIV/0!, #VALUE!, or #N/A)

- ✔ Text dates (that is, dates you format as text or precede with an apostrophe) that you enter with two-digit years

- ✔ Numbers that you store as text (that is, numbers that you format as text or precede with an apostrophe)

- ✔ Inconsistent formulas in a region (that is, formulas that are different from formulas in surrounding cells)

- ✔ Formulas that omit cells in a region (for example, a formula that sums a range but omits the last cell or cells in the range)

- ✔ Unlocked cells that contain formulas if the worksheet is protected

- ✔ Formulas that contain references to empty cells

Remember: Use Excel's suggestions to serve as a guide to potential errors in your worksheet. Excel may flag as errors data that you enter intentionally.

Excel's error-alert feature isn't foolproof. You should use it with other techniques that we discuss in this part.

Checking for errors in the background

By default, Excel checks for worksheet errors in the background. If it identifies an error or a potential error, Excel displays an indicator in the upper-left corner of the offending cell. After you click the cell, Excel displays the Error Warning Smart Tag on the left side of the offending cell. If you hover the mouse pointer over the Error Warning Smart Tag, Excel displays a message that indicates the nature of the error, as shown in Figure 7-1.

Figure 7-1

	B8	▾	f_x	=SUM(B4:B6)			
	A	B	C	D	E	F	G
1							
2			Department #3 2011 Budget				
3		Q1	Q2	Q3	Q4		
4	Salaries	$ 450,000.00	$ 450,000.00	$ 450,000.00	$ 450,000.00		
5	Travel	$ 3,200.00	$ 3,700.00	$ 3,500.00	$ 2,600.00		
6	Supplies	$ 500.00	$ 500.00	$ 500.00	$ 750.00		
7	Communications	$ 400.00	$ 450.00	$ 450.00	$ 700.00		
8	Total	$ 453,700.00	$ 454,650.00	$ 454,450.00	$ 454,050.00		
9							
10		The formula in this cell refers to a range that has additional numbers adjacent to it.					
11							

To correct the error or to tell Excel to ignore it, click the Error Warning Smart Tag and select an option from the drop-down list that appears.

See also "Checking for errors manually," immediately following this section.

Checking for errors manually

You may want to avoid the distraction of Excel's automatic worksheet error checking and perform the error-checking task manually after you complete work on your spreadsheet model.

To turn off background error checking, follow these steps:

1. Click the File tab and then click the Options button.

2. In the Excel Options dialog box, click the Formulas category.

3. In the Error Checking section, deselect the Enable Background Error Checking check box.

4. Click OK.

To check for worksheet errors manually, follow these steps:

1. Select the worksheet that you want to check for errors.

2. Click the Formulas tab on the Ribbon and then click the Error Checking button in the Formula Auditing group. Excel displays the Error Checking dialog box and places the cell pointer in the first cell that it encounters containing an error or potential error. The dialog box indicates the nature of the error that you encounter in the cell, as shown in Figure 7-2.

Figure 7-2

Error Checking	
Error in cell B8	Update Formula to Include Cells
=SUM(B4:B6)	Help on this error
Formula Omits Adjacent Cells	Ignore Error
The formula in this cell refers to a range that has additional numbers adjacent to it.	Edit in Formula Bar
Options...	Previous Next

3. Click one of the four option buttons on the right side of the dialog box.

4. Click Next to move to the next cell that contains an error or a potential error.

 An alternative to this procedure is to turn on background error checking *after* your spreadsheet model is complete and use the procedure in "Checking for errors in the background," immediately preceding this section, for each cell that Excel flags with an error.

You can control the types of errors that you want Excel to consider (automatically or through the manual procedure). Click the File tab and then click the Options button. Click the Formulas section on the left pane of the dialog box, and select or deselect the options in the Error Checking Rules area.

Checking Your Spelling

Excel uses a spell checker that works just like the feature you find in word-processing programs. You can access the spell checker by using either of the following methods:

- Click the Review tab on the Ribbon and then click the Spelling button.

- Press F7.

The extent of the spell checking depends on what you select before you access the dialog box.

What You Select	What Excel Checks
A single cell	The entire worksheet, including cell contents, notes, text in graphic objects and charts, and page headers and footers
A range of cells	Only that range
A group of characters	Only the characters in the formula bar

If Excel encounters a word that isn't in the current dictionary or is misspelled, it offers a list of suggestions that you can click to respond to.

Creating a Table of Names

You can create a list of all the names and associated name references in the workbook. This procedure may be useful for tracking down errors or as a way to document your work.

To create a table of names, follow these steps:

1. Move the cell pointer to an empty area of your worksheet or add a new worksheet. (Excel creates the table at the active cell position.)

2. Click the Formulas tab on the Ribbon, click the arrow on the Use in Formula button, and then select Paste Names at the bottom of the list. (Or simply press F3.) Excel displays the Paste Name dialog box.

3. Click the Paste List button and Excel creates your table of names.

The list that Excel pastes overwrites any cells that get in the way, so make sure the active cell is in an empty portion of the worksheet.

Displaying Formulas in a Worksheet

One way to audit your workbook is to display the formulas rather than the results of the formulas. Then you can examine the formulas without needing to select cells individually.

 To display formulas instead of formula results, click the Formulas tab on the Ribbon and then click the Show Formulas button in the Formula Auditing group. (You can also press Ctrl+~.)

 You may want to create a new window for the workbook before issuing this command. That way, you can see the formulas in one window and the results in the other. **See also** "Creating Multiple Windows (Views) for a Workbook," in Part 2.

Evaluating Parts of a Formula

Excel provides a tool that helps you evaluate (that is, calculate) parts of a formula and trace the precedents of parts of a formula. (*Precedents* are cells that are referenced in the formula part you're evaluating.) The capability to evaluate parts of a formula can prove useful if you're tracking down errors in formulas.

To evaluate parts of a formula, follow these steps:

1. Click the cell that contains the formula.

 2. Click the Formulas tab on the Ribbon and then click the Evaluate Formula button in the Formula Auditing group. Excel displays the Evaluate Formula dialog box. In the Reference area, the cell reference appears. The Evaluation preview box displays the formula with the first expression or cell reference underlined.

3. To show the value of the underlined expression, click Evaluate. Excel italicizes the result of the expression.

4. Repeat Step 3 as many times as necessary to evaluate all expressions in the formula.

5. Use the Step In button to examine the formula that the underlined cell reference in the expression represents. Use the Step Out button to evaluate the current reference and return to the previous reference (see Figure 7-3).

6. Click Close after you finish evaluating the formula.

Figure 7-3

Evaluate Formula dialog box:

Reference:		Evaluation:
Sheet5!$B$10	=	ABS(PMT(B3/12,B4,B8))
Sheet5!$B$3	=	B1
Sheet5!$B$1	=	6%

The cell currently being evaluated contains a constant.

Evaluate   Step In   **Step Out**   Close

Remember: The Step In button is not available if a cell reference is in a different workbook.

The Evaluate Formula feature is an excellent tool to use when your formula returns an error value because you can examine and correct the part of the formula that is generating the error.

A quick way to evaluate parts of a formula is to go into edit mode (by double-clicking the cell or pressing F2), highlight the part of the formula that you want to evaluate, and press F9. Excel displays the result of the formula part. Press Esc to cancel. Do *not* press Enter; otherwise, Excel permanently replaces the part of the formula with the resulting value.

Finding Specific Data

If your worksheets contain lots of data, you may find locating a particular piece of information difficult. Excel can find the data for you.

To locate a particular value or sequence of text, follow these steps:

1. Click the Find & Select button on the Ribbon's Home tab and choose Find from the menu. (Or simply press Ctrl+F.) Excel displays its Find and Replace dialog box with the Find tab selected, as shown in Figure 7-4.

Figure 7-4

Find and Replace dialog box:

Find | Replace

Find what: | | No Format Set | Format... |

Within: Sheet
Search: By Rows
Look in: Formulas

Match case
Match entire cell contents

Options <<

Find All   Find Next   Close

2. In the Find What drop-down list box, enter the characters to search for. You can use the list also to select items that you previously searched for.

3. If you want to make your search case-sensitive, select the Match Case check box. If the Match Case check box isn't visible, click the Options button.

4. To search for data with specific formatting:

    a. Click the Format button. (If the Format button isn't visible, click the Options button.) Excel displays the Find Format dialog box.

    b. Click the appropriate tabs, and in each tab, specify the formatting that you're looking for.

    c. After you complete your selections, click OK.

If a cell in your worksheet already contains all the formatting you want to use in your search, click the arrow on the Format button and select Choose Format From Cell. Excel adds an eyedropper icon to the cursor. Click the cell with the required formatting.

5. In the Within drop-down list box, select whether you want to look in the active sheet or the entire workbook. (If the Within drop-down box isn't visible, click the Options button.)

6. In the Search drop-down box, select the direction that you want to search, as follows:

    - Select By Rows to search across rows.

    - Select By Columns to search down columns.

    In most cases, your search goes faster if you select By Columns.

7. In the Look In drop-down list box, specify what to look in: Formulas, Values, or Comments.

8. Click the Find Next or Find All button. If you click Find Next, Excel selects the cell that contains what you're looking for. If you click the Find All button, Excel displays a drop-down window that shows all references to the found data, either in the active worksheet or across the entire workbook, depending on your selection in Step 5. Click a reference in the window to go directly to that cell.

9. Click the Close button to end your search.

For approximate searches, use *wildcard characters.* An asterisk represents any group of characters in the specified position, and a question mark represents any single character in the specified position. If you type **w*h**, for example, those letters represent all text that begins with *w* and ends with *h*. Similarly, **b?n** matches three-letter words such as *bin, bun,* and *ban.*

Remember: To find a cell or cells with specific formatting but containing no specific data, you can skip Step 2.

See also "Searching for Data to Replace," in Part 4.

Handling Circular References

As you enter formulas, you may occasionally see a message from Excel that is similar to the one shown in Figure 7-5. This message indicates that the formula you just entered will result in a circular reference. A *circular reference* occurs if a formula refers to its own value (either directly or indirectly).

Figure 7-5

Microsoft Office Excel

Circular Reference Warning

One or more formulas contain a circular reference and may not calculate correctly. Circular references are any references within a formula that depend upon the results of that same formula. For example, a cell that refers to its own value or a cell that refers to another cell which depends on the original cell's value both contain circular references.

For more information about understanding, finding, and removing circular references, click OK. If you want to create a circular reference, click Cancel to continue.

OK   Cancel

If Excel encounters a circular reference after you enter a formula, a message is displayed that enables you to correct the formula or to enter the formula as is. If you enter a formula with a circular reference, Excel displays a message in the status bar to remind you that a circular reference exists. Most of the time, a circular reference indicates an error that you must correct. In this case, you should click OK after Excel displays the message.

After you click OK in response to the circular reference message, Excel displays direct and indirect *precedent* arrows on the worksheet that loop back to the cell with the circular reference. These arrows help you trace the path of the circular reference. Excel also displays a help window, which provides further assistance for locating circular reference problems. Excel also displays the help viewer (help window), which displays help topics specific to working with circular references.

If you receive a workbook containing circular references, Excel displays a message on the status bar, as mentioned. To correct the problem, follow these steps:

1. Click the Formulas tab on the Ribbon.

2. In the Formula Auditing group, click the arrow on the Error Checking button, and then choose Circular References from the menu. Excel displays a list that includes the cell reference of the cell with the circular reference and the references of any other cells involved in the circular reference (see Figure 7-6).

Figure 7-6

3. Click a cell reference in the list. Excel positions the active cell pointer in the cell.

4. To trace the path of the circular reference, click the Trace Precedents button on the Formulas tab on the Ribbon. Excel displays an arrow on the worksheet that points from the direct precedent of the cell.

5. Click the Trace Precedents button again to add the first indirect precedent of the cell (that is, the precedent of the direct precedent), click again to add the second indirect precedent (that is, the precedent of the first indirect precedent), and so on. Eventually, the precedent arrows loop back to the cell with the circular reference.

The trace precedents technique can be helpful in resolving many circular reference problems.

See also "Tracing Cell Relationships," later in this part.

After you resolve the circular reference problem for a cell, if additional cells have circular reference problems, Excel continues to display the circular reference message on the status bar.

Excel doesn't tell you about a circular reference if the Iteration setting is on. You can check this setting by clicking the File tab, clicking the Options button, and then clicking the Formulas option section in the left pane. The Enable Iterative Calculation option is in the Calculation Options area on the right side of the dialog box. If iteration is on (that is, the Enable Iterative Calculation option is selected), Excel performs the circular calculation the number of times specified in the Maximum Iterations text box (or until the value changes by less than 0.001 — or whatever value is in the Maximum Change text box).

Remember: In a few situations (known by advanced users), a circular reference is intentional. In these cases, the iteration setting must be on. However, it's best to keep the iteration setting off so that Excel warns you of circular references.

Locating Errors by Selecting Special Cells

Excel's ability to select specific types of cells can prove useful in your auditing work. For example, you can select all cells in the worksheet that contain formulas. (Excel highlights all such cells.) If Excel doesn't select a cell in a region where it highlights other cells (for example, a formula row or column), that situation may indicate that you (or someone else) inadvertently overwrote the cell with a static value.

Follow these steps to select cells that meet your criterion:

1. Click the Find & Select button on the Ribbon's Home tab and then choose an option in the middle part of the menu. The choices are Formulas, Comments, Conditional Formatting, Constants, and Data Validation. Excel highlights all the cells matching the criterion you chose.

2. For additional criteria choices:

    a. Choose Go To Special on the Find & Select button menu. Excel displays the Go To Special dialog box.

    b. Select an option in the Go To Special dialog box.

    c. To get help on the options in the dialog box, click the help button (the question mark icon) in the dialog box title bar. Excel displays a help window. Click OK to close the window.

3. Click OK. Excel selects all cells that match your selected criteria.

To get an overall view of the worksheet structure if you're selecting special cells and to aid in tracking down potential errors, zoom out the worksheet to a small size. ***See*** "Zooming a Worksheet," in Part 3.

Excel has some shortcut keys that you can use to select precedent and dependent cells without needing to use the Go To Special dialog box.

Key Combination	What It Selects
Ctrl+[	Direct precedents
Ctrl+Shift+[	All precedents
Ctrl+]	Direct dependents
Ctrl+Shift+]	All dependents

See also "Tracing Cell Relationships," next.

Tracing Cell Relationships

Excel's auditing tools can help you track down errors in your worksheet by drawing arrows (known as *cell tracers*) to precedent and dependent cells. A cell's *direct precedents* are cells that are referenced in the cell's formula. An *indirect precedent* is a cell that isn't used directly in the formula but is used by a cell that you refer to in the formula. A cell's *dependents* are formulas that reference the particular cell, either directly or indirectly.

Tracing precedents and dependents

To trace the precedents or dependents of a cell, follow these steps:

1. Click the cell that you want to trace.

2. Click the Formulas tab on the Ribbon and do one of the following:

    - Click the Trace Precedents button in the Formula Auditing group. Excel draws arrows from all *direct* precedent cells.

    - Click the Trace Dependents button in the Formula Auditing group. Excel draws arrows to all *direct* dependent cells. See an example in Figure 7-7.

Figure 7-7

3. Repeat Step 2 (click the Trace Precedent or Trace Dependent button) as often as necessary to draw arrows to *indirect* precedent or *indirect* dependent cells.

4. Double-click an arrow to move the cell pointer to a precedent cell or a dependent cell. If Excel displays a dashed line pointing to a miniature sheet icon, the precedent cells are on a different worksheet. Double-clicking the dashed line displays the Go To dialog box. Click a cell reference in the Go To dialog box and then click OK.

5. Click the Formulas tab on the Ribbon (if necessary) and then click the Remove Arrows button in the Formula Auditing group after you finish tracing the source of your error.

If you are developing a large worksheet, this type of interactive tracing is often more revealing if you zoom out of the worksheet to display a larger area. **See** "Zooming a Worksheet," in Part 3.

See also "Tracing formula error values," immediately following this section.

Tracing formula error values

Often, an error in one cell (for example, #DIV/0!, #VALUE!, or #NA) is the result of an error in a precedent cell. Excel helps you to identify the cell or cells that are causing the error value to appear.

To trace the source of the error value, follow these steps:

1. Click the cell that contains the error.

2. Click the Formulas tab on the Ribbon, click the arrow on the Error Checking button in the Formula Auditing group, and choose Trace Error from the menu. Excel draws arrows to all *direct* precedent cells.

3. Repeat Step 2 as often as necessary to draw arrows to *indirect* precedent cells.

4. Double-click an arrow to move the cell pointer to a precedent cell.

5. Click the Formulas tab on the Ribbon (if necessary) and click the Remove Arrows button in the Formula Auditing group after you finish tracing the source of your error.

See also "Understanding Formula Error Values," which appears next, and "Tracing precedents and dependents," earlier in this section.

Understanding Formula Error Values

Excel flags errors in formulas with a message that begins with a pound sign (#). This flag signals that the formula is returning an error value. You must correct the formula (or correct a cell that the formula references) to get rid of the error display.

Remember: If the entire cell is full of pound signs, the column isn't wide enough to display the value (whether or not the value is an error).

The following table lists the types of error values that may appear in a cell that contains a formula.

Error Value	Explanation
#DIV/0!	The formula is trying to divide by zero (an operation that's not allowed on this planet). This error also occurs if the formula attempts to divide by an empty cell.
#NAME?	The formula uses a name that Excel doesn't recognize. This error can happen if you delete a name that the formula uses or if you have unmatched quotes when using text.
#N/A	The error will occur, for example, if the formula refers (directly or indirectly) to a cell that uses #N/A or the NA() function to signal that data is not available. The error might also appear if a required argument is omitted from a worksheet function. A complete discussion of all the possible causes of this error is beyond the scope of this book.
#NULL!	The formula uses an intersection of two ranges that don't intersect.
#NUM!	You have a problem with a value; for example, you're specifying a negative number where Excel expects a positive number.
#REF!	The formula refers to a cell that isn't valid. This error can happen if you've deleted the cell from the worksheet.
#VALUE!	The formula contains a function with an invalid argument, or the formula uses an operand of the wrong type (such as text where Excel expects a value).

Remember: A single error value can make its way to lots of other cells that contain formulas that depend on the cell.

See also "Tracing formula error values," earlier in this part.

Using Cell Comments

The Excel Cell Comment feature enables you to attach a comment to a cell. Comments are useful for documenting a particular value, providing input instructions for users, or helping you remember what a formula does. After you move the mouse pointer over a cell that has a comment, the comment appears in a small box (see Figure 7-8).

Figure 7-8

Adding a cell comment

To add a comment to a cell, follow these steps:

1. Select the cell.

2. Click the Review tab on the Ribbon and then click the New Comment button. (You can also right-click the cell and choose New Comment from the contextual menu, or press Shift+F2.)

3. In the text box, enter the text for the comment.

4. After you finish, click any cell.

The cell displays a small red triangle to indicate that it contains a comment.

Editing a cell comment

To edit a comment, follow these steps:

1. Select the cell containing the comment.

2. Click the Review tab on the Ribbon and then click the Edit Comment button. (You can also right-click the cell and choose Edit Comment from the contextual menu, or press Shift+F2.)

3. Edit your comment in the text box displayed.

4. After you finish, click any cell.

Viewing cell comments

Cells to which you attach a comment display a small red triangle in the upper-right corner. After you move the mouse pointer over a cell that contains a comment, Excel displays the comment.

To view all the comments in the worksheet, click the Review tab on the Ribbon and then click the Show All Comments button. Click Show All Comments again to remove the comment display.

TIP

Zoom out of your worksheet to view more comments. *See* "Zooming a Worksheet," in Part 3.

Using the Watch Window

If you're attempting to track down certain problems with large spreadsheet models, the capability to display a window that shows the value of the formula cells if their associated precedents are in different parts of a worksheet, in different worksheets, or even in different open workbooks comes in handy. For example, this ability can be useful if you're unsure of the results that Excel is generating in certain formula cells after you change the values in precedent cells (that is, the cells that the formula references either directly or indirectly). This way, if you make changes to precedent cells, you can see the result of formulas immediately in the window. Excel provides a *Watch window* to handle these situations.

Displaying and adding cells to the Watch window

To display and add cells to the Watch window, follow these steps:

1. Select the cells that you want to watch.

2. Click the Formulas tab on the Ribbon and then click the Watch Window button in the Formula Auditing group. Excel displays the Watch window.

3. Click Add Watch. Excel displays the Add Watch dialog box, with the cell references that you selected in Step 1 already filled in.

4. Click the Add button. Excel adds the cell references to the Watch window, as shown in Figure 7-9.

Figure 7-9

Watch Window ▾ ×
🔾 Add Watch...   🔾 Delete Watch

Book	Sheet	Name	Cell	Value	Formula
Sales Commissions...	Master	CommissionAmt	AA6	$2.47	=IF(H6="ERROR","#NA",SUM(OFFSET(Extended_Price,ROW()-ROW(Extended_Price),3,1,COLUMN()-COLUMN(Extended_Price)-3))
Sales Commissions...	Control ...	EndDate	AG29	30-Jun-07	=IF(AF29="",DATE(YEAR(TODAY()),12,31),AF29)
Sales Commissions...	Control ...	CommissionRate	AC42	0.03	=INDEX($AE$29:$AE$38,MATCH(1,($AE$40>=$AC$29:$AC$38)*($AC$40=$AD$29:$AD$38)*($AE$40<=$AG$29:$AG$38),0))

5. To move the active cell pointer to the cell that an entry in the Watch window refers to, double-click the entry in the window.

6. To add cells from other worksheets or open workbooks, switch to the other worksheet or workbook and repeat Steps 1–4.

7. To close or hide the Watch window, click the Close button or click the Watch Window button on the Ribbon's Formula tab.

TIP Instead of closing the Watch window, you can choose to dock it to one side of the screen. Click the title bar of the Watch window and then drag the window to any side of the screen.

To change the width of a column in the Watch window, drag the boundary on the right side of the column heading (the mouse pointer changes to a cross with a double-sided arrow). To resize the Watch window, drag any side of the window (the mouse pointer turns into a double-sided arrow.)

Remember: Cells that contain links to other workbooks appear in the Watch window only if the other workbooks are open.

TIP To select all the cells in a worksheet that contain formulas, do the following: In Step 1, click the Find & Select button on the Ribbon's Home tab, choose Go To Special from the menu, select Formulas in the Go To Special dialog box that appears, and click OK.

Removing cells from the Watch window

To remove cells from the Watch window, follow these steps:

1. Select the cell references in the Watch window that you want to remove. To select contiguous cell references, click the first reference, press and hold Shift, and click the last reference. To select noncontiguous references, press Ctrl and then click the cells.

2. Click Delete Watch.

Formatting Your Data

You have a lot of control over the appearance of information that you enter into a cell. Changing the appearance of a cell's content is known as *formatting*. Formatting data in a range can make your worksheet more readable and presentable. In this part, you discover how to apply Excel's many formatting options.

In this part . . .

- ✔ **Changing the Appearance of Cell Contents**
- ✔ **Formatting Based on the Contents of a Cell or Range**
- ✔ **Formatting Numbers**
- ✔ **Formatting Ranges Using Comparative Visualizations**
- ✔ **Using Cell Styles**

Adding Borders to a Cell or a Range

People often use borders to group a range of similar cells or simply as a way to delineate rows or columns for aesthetic purposes.

To add borders around a cell or range, follow these steps:

1. Select the cell or range.

2. Click the arrow on the Borders button on the Ribbon's Home tab. Excel displays the Borders menu.

3. Choose a border style from the menu. Excel applies the border to your selection. In addition, the Borders button icon changes to reflect your border selection.

If the available styles on the menu aren't what you want, follow these steps to select further options:

1. At the bottom of the Borders menu, choose More Borders. Excel displays the Format Cells dialog box with the Borders tab selected.

2. If you want to change the default color, choose a color for the border from the Color drop-down palette.

3. In the Style area of the dialog box, select a line style.

4. Select the border position(s) for the line style by clicking in the Text window or by clicking one or more buttons surrounding the Text window. To deselect a line in the Text window, click the line. Note that you can apply diagonal borders that extend through cells and ranges. Diagonal borders give the effect of the cells being "crossed out."

5. Click OK to apply the border(s) to your selection.

TIP If you use border formatting in your worksheet, you may want to turn off the grid display to make the borders more pronounced. Click the View tab on the Ribbon and then click the Gridlines option to remove its check mark.

Aligning Cell Contents

Excel's default alignments are such that cell contents appear at the bottom, numbers are right-aligned, text is left-aligned, and logical values (True or False) are centered in cells. You can use Excel's alignment tools to change the default alignments that Excel applies to cell contents. Figure 8-1 shows several alignment options discussed in this section.

Figure 8-1

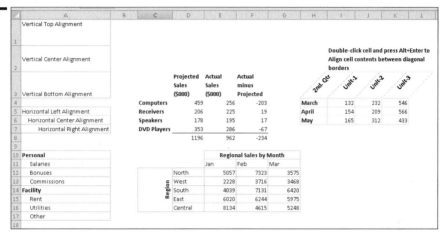

To apply a standard alignment option, select the cell or range that you want to align and then select one of the following options from the Alignment group on the Ribbon's Home tab. (Hover the mouse pointer over an alignment option to display an Extended ScreenTip for the option.)

- ✔ **Vertical alignment:** The options are Top, Center, and Bottom. See cells A1:A3 in Figure 8-1.

- ✔ **Horizontal alignment**: The options are Left, Center, and Right. See cells A5:A7 in Figure 8-1.

- ✔ **Indent:** The options are Increase Indent and Decrease Indent. Multiple clicks on the Increase Indent or Decrease Indent buttons increase or decrease the indent further. See cells A11:A13 and A15:A17 in Figure 8-1.

- ✔ **Orientation:** Click the Orientation button to display a menu of predefined orientations. Excel adjusts the row height to display the text. If you don't want this adjustment, you can use the Merge feature first (described shortly) to avoid a larger row height across the worksheet. See cells H3:K3 in Figure 8-1.

- ✔ **Wrap Text:** Select this option when you want a long text entry to take up less horizontal area on the worksheet. See cells D3:F3 in Figure 8-1.

- ✔ **Merge and Center:** You can merge multiple cells into a single, larger cell. This feature enables you to have cells of unequal sizes. If you have a table that spans six columns, for example, you can merge six cells at the top to form a single larger cell for the table's title. In Figure 8-1, cells E10:G10 are merged horizontally, and cells C12:C15 are merged vertically. Note the following rules when merging cells:

- You can merge cells horizontally or vertically.

- If a selection contains more than one nonempty cell, the merged cells contain the contents and formatting of the upper-left cell of the merged range.

- Understanding that *cells* are merged — not the *contents* of cells — is important. Whenever you merge cells, you receive a warning if the selected range contains more than one nonempty cell.

If you do not want to center your data when you merge cells, or if you want to unmerge cells, click the arrow on the Merge and Center button and then choose the appropriate option on the menu.

Changing the Appearance of Cell Contents

By default, Excel formats the information you enter into a worksheet by using the 11-point Calibri font. However, if you want to emphasize various parts of your worksheet, such as the headers in a list, you can apply a different font style, size, color, background, or attribute to the header cells.

To apply a standard formatting option, select the cell or range that you want to format and then select one of the following options from the Format group on the Ribbon's Home tab:

✔ **Font Face:** Select a font face from the font picker drop-down list. To preview the change in the selected cell or range before you commit to the change, hover the mouse pointer over a font face in the list.

✔ **Font Size:** Select a font size from the font picker drop-down list. To preview the change in the selected cell or range before you commit to the change, hover the mouse pointer over a font size in the list.

✔ **Increase/Decrease Font Size:** These buttons increase or decrease the font in the selected cell or range by 1 or 2 points.

✔ **Font Style:** The options are Bold, Italic and Underline. Click the arrow on the Underline button if you want to apply a double-underline to the contents of your selected cell or range.

You can also use the following shortcut keys to apply a standard font style to your selection: Ctrl+B for bold, Ctrl+I for italic, and Ctrl+U for underline.

Remember: The Ribbon buttons and shortcut keys act as toggles. You can turn bold on and off, for example, by repeatedly pressing Ctrl+B (or clicking the Bold button).

✔ **Font Color:** Click the Font Color button to apply the color that the button displays to the font in your selected cell or range. Click the arrow on the button to choose a color from the color palette.

✔ **Background Color:** Click the Background Color button to apply the cell background color that the button displays. Click the arrow on the button to select a color from the color palette.

Remember: If you choose fonts or colors that are part of a theme, the fonts or colors change if you change the workbook theme. ***See*** "Formatting with Themes," in Part 1 for a discussion of theme fonts and colors and "Using Cell Styles," later in this part.

Copying Formats

The quickest way to copy the formats from one cell to another cell or range is to use the Format Painter button on the Ribbon's Home tab. Follow these steps:

1. Select the cell or range with the formatting attributes that you want to copy.

2. Click the Format Painter button. Note that the mouse pointer appears as a miniature paintbrush.

3. Select (paint) the cells to which you want to apply the formats.

4. Release the mouse button, and Excel copies the formats.

TIP Double-clicking the Format Painter button causes the mouse pointer to remain a paintbrush after you release the mouse button. This paintbrush enables you to paint other areas of the worksheet with the same formats. To exit paint mode, click the Format Painter button again (or press Esc).

Formatting Based on the Contents of a Cell or Range

In addition to applying static formatting to your worksheet cells and ranges, you can format a cell or range based on the contents of the cell or range. Using Excel's *conditional formatting* feature, you can format one or more cells based on the values in the cells, or you can format a range based on the relative values of the cells in the range. You may, for example, want to visually identify all cells in a range that exceed a certain value or you may want to highlight cells in a range having duplicate values.

You can apply any combination of the following standard formatting options when the criteria for formatting the cell are met: Number, Font, Border, and Fill. ***See also*** "Changing the Appearance of Cell Contents," earlier in this part.

Formatting based on individual cell values

Excel provides several criteria that you can use to format individual cells. You can format cells based on

- ✔ The value in the cell.

- ✔ A formula. The formula must return a value of True or False for the condition to be applied. For example, to apply a format to cell C3 if the sum of the values in cells A1 to A10 is greater than 2500, you enter the following conditional formula for cell C3:

  ```
  =SUM($A$1:$A$10)>2500
  ```

  The formula returns True if the sum of cells A1 to A10 is greater than 2500 and False otherwise.

In Excel 2010, your conditional formatting formulas can contain references to cells or ranges in a worksheet other than the one in which the formatting has been applied.

- ✔ The cells containing, not containing, beginning with, or ending with specific text. In a list of parts, for example, you can highlight part numbers that contain certain characters.

- ✔ The cells containing dates that match dynamic conditions, such as yesterday, today, tomorrow, in the last 7 days, last week, this week, next week, last month, this month, or next month. Excel calculates the date based on your PC's internal real-time clock, so you do not have to update the condition manually.

- ✔ The cells being blank or nonblank.

- ✔ The cells having or not having errors.

Follow these steps to conditionally format individual cells or a range of cells:

1. Select the cell or range that you want to format conditionally.

2. Click the Conditional Formatting button on the Ribbon's Home tab. Excel displays a menu of conditional formatting options.

3. Choose Highlight Cells Rules and then choose any option except Duplicate Values from the flyout menu. For example, to format a cell or range of cells if the values in the cells exceed a certain value, choose Greater Than from the flyout menu.

4. In the dialog box that appears (see Figure 8-2), enter a value (or values in the case of Between) in the box on the left. (The label for this box changes depending on what you chose in Step 3.) Instead of entering a value in the Format Cells That Are box, you can click the mouse pointer in the box and point to a cell on the worksheet.

Figure 8-2

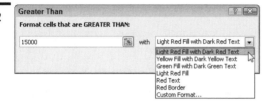

5. If you see a formatting option you like in the drop-down list on the right, select the option and then click OK to apply the conditional format.

6. If you don't like any of the available formatting options:

   a. Select Custom Format at the bottom of the drop-down list. Excel displays the Format Cells dialog box.

   b. Select your formatting options on the Number, Font, Border, and Fill tabs as appropriate.

   c. Click OK to close the Format Cells dialog box, and then click OK again to apply the conditional format.

Remember: If the cell doesn't meet the condition that you specify, it takes on the standard formatting for the cell.

If you copy a cell containing conditional formatting, the conditional formatting applies to all copies.

Formatting based on values in a range

Excel 2010 provides several criteria that you can use to format cells based on a comparison of the cell values in a range. You can format cells in a range based on

- Duplicate or unique values
- Top N items (values), where N is a number you specify
- Top N% rank, where N is a number you specify
- Bottom N items (values), where N is a number you specify
- Bottom N% rank, where N is a number you specify
- Above average values

✔ Below average values

✔ Average or above average values

✔ Average or below average values

✔ One to three standard deviations above average values

✔ One to three standard deviations below average values

Follow these steps to conditionally format a range of cells based on a comparison of the cells in the range:

1. Select the range that you want to format conditionally.

2. Click the Conditional Formatting button on the Ribbon's Home tab. Excel displays a menu of conditional formatting options.

3. Choose one of the following options:

   • To highlight duplicate or unique values in the range, choose Highlight Cells Rules and then choose Duplicate Values from the flyout menu.

   • To highlight the top N value cells, top N% rank cells, and so on, choose Top/Bottom Rules and then choose an option in the flyout menu.

4. In the dialog box that appears (see Figure 8-3 for an example), select the value option on the left side.

Figure 8-3

5. If you see a formatting option you like in the drop-down list, select the option and click OK to apply the conditional format.

6. If you don't like any of the available formatting options:

   a. Select Custom Format at the bottom of the list. Excel displays the Format Cells dialog box.

   b. Choose your formatting options on the Number, Font, Border, and Fill tabs as appropriate.

   c. Click OK to close the Format Cells dialog box, and then click OK again to apply the conditional format.

Applying multiple conditional formats to a cell or range

Excel allows you to specify more than one conditional format for a cell. For example, you can have different formatting for a cell based on the value in the cell.

In Excel 2007 and later, the number of conditional formats per cell is limited only by your PC's memory. Also, Excel 2010 allows you to apply multiple conditional formats to a cell if more than one condition is True. For example, if one conditional format applies a bold font when a formatting condition is True, and another makes the cell background color red when a second formatting condition is True, Excel applies both formats to the cell if the two conditions evaluate to True. If the formatting conflicts (for example, a red font and a green font), Excel applies only the first rule that meets the condition.

Follow these steps to add an additional conditional format for a cell or range:

1. Select the cell or range that already contains one conditional format.

2. Click the Conditional Formatting button on the Ribbon's Home tab and choose Manage Rules (at the bottom of the menu). Excel displays the Conditional Formatting Rules Manager dialog box, as shown in Figure 8-4.

Figure 8-4

By default, the window in the bottom portion of the dialog box displays the conditional formatting rule(s) applied to the current selection. If you weren't sure of the range in Step 1, you can click the Show Formatting Rules For drop-down list and select This Worksheet (or other worksheets in the workbook). The rules window then displays all the conditional formatting rules and the ranges to which the rule(s) apply. Make note of the range to which you want to add a new rule, exit the dialog box, and begin again at Step 1.

3. In the dialog box, click the New Rule button. Excel displays the New Formatting Rule dialog box.

4. In the Select a Rule Type list, choose a rule type. To apply standard conditional formatting options (number, font, border, or patterns), do *not* select the first option in the window (Format All Cells Based on Their Values). The controls that appear initially in the Edit the Rules Description section depend on the rule type you chose.

5. In the leftmost drop-down list in the Edit the Rules Description section, choose an option (for all choices in Step 4 except Use a Formula to Determine Which Cells to Format). New controls appear to the right of this drop-down list depending on your choice. Complete the requirements for the controls (for example, enter a value, enter a cell reference, or choose from a list).

6. Click Format to display the Format Cells dialog box and select your formatting options from among the available tabs.

7. Click OK to exit the dialog box, and click OK again to exit the New Formatting Rule dialog box. Excel returns you to the Conditional Formatting Rules Manager dialog box.

8. Excel evaluates conditional formatting rules in the order listed in the Conditional Formatting Rules Manager dialog box. To change the evaluation order of a rule, select the rule and click the up or down arrow to the right of the Delete Rule button.

9. Click OK.

Editing or deleting a conditional format

Follow these steps if you want to edit a condition for a cell or range or delete a condition for a cell or range with multiple conditions:

1. Select the cell or range that contains the conditional format you want to edit or delete.

2. Click the Conditional Formatting button on the Ribbon's Home tab, and then choose Manage Rules (at the bottom of the menu). Excel displays the Conditional Formatting Rules Manager dialog box.

3. In the Conditional Formatting Rules Manager dialog box, select the condition you want to edit or delete.

4. Do one of the following:

   • To delete the condition, click Delete.

   • To edit the condition, click Edit. Make your changes in the Edit Formatting Rule dialog box that appears and then click OK.

5. Click OK.

To quickly delete (clear) all conditional formatting rules for a cell or range, select the cell or range, click the Conditional Formatting button on the Ribbon's Home tab, choose Clear Rules from the menu, and then choose Selected Cells from the flyout menu. To quickly delete (clear) all conditional formatting rules for the active worksheet, choose Entire Sheet from the Clear Rules flyout menu.

Formatting a Number

Excel internally stores all numbers and dates that you enter in your worksheet as plain, unformatted numbers. You can use Excel's built-in numeric and date/time formats to make your data more readable and understandable. In addition, if you can't find a suitable built-in format to fit your needs, you can create a custom number format.

Using Excel's built-in number formats

Excel is smart enough to perform some number formatting for you automatically. If you enter **9.6%** into a cell, for example, Excel knows that you want to use a percentage format and applies it for you automatically. Similarly, if you use commas to separate thousands (such as **123,456**) or a dollar sign to indicate currency (such as **$123.45**), Excel applies the appropriate formatting for you.

Use the buttons in the Number group on the Ribbon's Home tab to quickly apply common number formats. After you click one of these buttons, the active cell takes on the specified number format.

$ ▾ You can select among several currency symbols by clicking the arrow on the Accounting Number Format button in the Number group on the Ribbon's Home tab and choosing a symbol from the menu.

To access additional number formats, click the arrow on the Number Format drop-down list above the number format buttons and select an option from the list.

If none of the predefined number format buttons or Number Format list options fit the bill, you need to use the Format Cells dialog box. Follow these steps to select an option from the Format Cells dialog box:

1. Select a cell or range of cells you want to format.

2. Click the arrow on the Number Format drop-down list and select More Number Formats at the bottom of the list; or click the Number dialog launcher button at the bottom right of the Number group container. Excel displays the Format Cells dialog box with the Number tab selected.

3. In the Category list box, select one of the categories. After you choose a category, the right side of the dialog box changes to display the appropriate options.

4. Choose an option from the right side of the dialog box. The top of the dialog box displays a sample of how the active cell appears with the number format you chose.

5. Click OK to apply the number format to all the selected cells.

Remember: If the cell displays a series of pound signs (such as ####), it means the column isn't wide enough to display the value using the number format you chose. The solution is to make the column wider or to change the number format. ***See*** "Changing column width," later in this part.

Creating custom number formats

Excel provides many predefined number formats, but if none of these formats are satisfactory, you need to create a custom number format. Just follow these steps:

1. Complete Steps 1 to 3 for accessing the Format Cells dialog box as detailed in the preceding section, but in Step 3, select Custom in the Category list box.

2. Construct a number format by selecting an option from the list box on the right or by specifying a series of codes in the Type text box (located above the list box). In the Type text box, you can also modify a code you select from the list box. The Sample area shows how an entry in the active cell will be displayed with the code specified in the Type text box.

3. Click OK to store the custom number format and apply it to the selected cells. The custom number format is now available for you to use with other cells in the workbook.

To find out more about the meaning of custom formatting codes, check out this online resource:

```
http://office.microsoft.com/en-us/assistance/HP051986791033.
aspx
```

After reviewing the online information, it will become clearer how Excel constructs its built-in number formats. Click a cell with a built-in format, and then display the Format Cells dialog box as already described and select the custom option in the Category list box. The text box on the right of the dialog box displays the formatting code for the built-in format. If you want, you can create a custom format by modifying a built-in format.

Remember: Excel stores custom number formats with the workbook. To make the custom format available in a different workbook, you must copy a cell that uses the custom format to the other workbook.

Formatting a Range Using Comparative Visualizations

Comparative Visualizations allow you to compare the relative values in a range visually. Excel uses special conditional formatting within the cells to make this relative comparison. Visual comparisons are particularly useful if you have a lot of data to analyze because you can quickly detect anomalies, spot outliers (a value far from most others in a data set), compare performance (good, bad, or neutral), and so on. Excel provides the following three special conditional formatting tools for comparing the relative values in a range:

✔ **Data bar:** Uses horizontal bars to compare the relative sizes of values in the range.

✔ **Color scale:** Uses color gradients (such as various shades of red, amber, and green) to compare the variation of values in the range.

✔ **Icon set:** Uses a set of icons (for example, up, down, and horizontal arrows) to compare values in the range.

Figure 8-5 shows examples of each visualization type.

Figure 8-5

Using a visualization to compare values in a range

To use a visualization to compare relative values in a range, follow these steps:

1. Select the range.

2. Click the Conditional Formatting button on the Ribbon's Home tab. Excel displays a menu of conditional formatting options.

3. Choose one of the following options from the menu:

- **Data Bars:** Choose a bar color from the flyout menu. By default, Excel uses the highest and lowest values in the range to draw the longest and shortest bar, respectively.

Excel 2010 provides a choice of bars with a gradient fill or a solid fill — either with or without a border. Also in Excel 2010, data bars are proportional to the corresponding cell values. A zero value in a cell displays no bar, and negative values can display bars in a direction opposite to that of positive value bars.

The data bar behavior in Excel 2010 is different from that in Excel 2007. In Excel 2007, the lengths of the bars were *not* proportional to the corresponding cell values. For example, a zero value displayed a bar, and negative values displayed bars in the same direction as positive values. In Excel 2007, you could not use the bars to compare values in the cell range.

- **Color Scales:** Choose a color scale from the flyout menu. By default, Excel uses the lowest, highest, and midpoint values in the range to determine the color gradients.

- **Icon Sets:** Choose an icon set from the flyout menu. You can choose icon sets having three, four, or five icons. By default, Excel uses percentages to determine the threshold between icons. In the case of a three-icon set, for example, Excel sets 33% and 67% as the thresholds between the three icons.

In Excel 2010, you can mix icons from different sets and choose whether or not to display an icon for each threshold in the range of numbers. For example, you may decide to display an icon only when the values in a range are below a specific threshold.

If you hover the mouse pointer over an option in a flyout menu, Excel shows a preview of the visualization that will be applied to the range.

Modifying the visualization for a range

After you create a visualization for a range, you can modify the visualization in several ways. You can use a different visualization, change the type of comparison among the values in the range, or display the visualization without the cell values.

Follow these steps to modify the visualization for a range:

1. Select the range that contains the visualization you want to edit.

2. Click the Conditional Formatting button on the Ribbon's Home tab and then choose Manage Rules (at the bottom of the menu). Excel displays the Conditional Formatting Rules Manager dialog box.

3. In the Conditional Formatting Rules Manager dialog box, click the Edit Rule button. If you have more than one conditional formatting rule applied to a range, select the rule you want to modify in the window before clicking the Edit Rule button. Excel displays the Edit Formatting Rule dialog box. See Figure 8-6.

Figure 8-6

4. In the Select a Rule Type list, ensure that Format All Cells Based on Their Values is selected.

5. To change the visualization in the selected range, select a new option in the Format Style drop-down list.

6. If you want a different comparison for the relative values in the range, first make a selection in the Type drop-down list. The options are Lowest or Highest value (applicable to data bars and color scales), Number, Percent, Percentile, and Formula.

7. Next, enter values for the type of comparison you chose. The Value option is not available if you choose Lowest Value or Highest Value for the comparison type. The values you enter have different meaning for the visualization you chose. For data bars, the values and comparison type combine to determine the bar length for each value in the selected range. For color scales, the values and comparison type combine to determine the color assigned to each value in the selected range. For icon sets, the values and comparison type combine to determine the icon assigned to each value in the selected range.

8. Select display options depending on the type of visualization you selected in Step 5 (Data bar, Color scale, or Icon set):

Data bars: Select bar appearance options from the appropriate drop-down boxes. You can change Fill (gradient or solid), Color, Border (no border or solid border), Border Color (for solid border), and Bar Direction (context, left-to-right, or right-to-left).

Click the Negative Value and Axis button to display the Negative Value and Axis dialog box. From here, you can change the fill color and border color for negative value bars, and the position of the axis in the cells, which is used to delineate negative and positive value bars. You can choose to display no axis, in which case both positive and negative bars are in the same direction (not the best choice in most cases). Click OK to return to the previous dialog box.

Color scales: Select colors for the lowest, highest, and midpoint values (3-color scale only).

Icon sets: Choose a "base" set from the Icon Style drop-down gallery. If you want to change the icon display choice for a value rule, click the appropriate Icon drop-down arrow on the left of the appropriate rule. Next select a new icon from the gallery, or select No Cell Icon.

If you want to display data bars or icons in the selected range without the associated values, select the Show Bar Only or Show Icon Only check box (available after you choose a data bar or icon set format style, respectively).

9. Click OK to return to the Rules Manager dialog box, and then click OK to exit and apply your changes.

Hiding Cell Contents

You can hide the contents of a cell by using either of the following formatting options:

- Apply a custom number format consisting of three semicolons (; ; ;). **See** "Creating custom number formats," earlier in this part.

- Make the text color the same as the background color. **See** "Changing the Appearance of Cell Contents," earlier in this part.

Both formatting techniques have the same flaw: If the active cell pointer is on the cell, its contents are visible in the formula bar. To avoid this flaw and make the cell contents truly invisible, you should protect the worksheet after you choose one of the preceding options. **See also** "Protecting a Worksheet," in Part 3.

Hiding and Unhiding Columns and Rows

Hiding columns and rows is useful if you don't want users to see particular information or if you don't want some information to print. Alternatively, you can unhide rows or columns to reveal information.

Hiding columns and rows

To hide one or more columns or rows, choose one of the following options:

- Select any cell(s) on the worksheet in the column(s) or row(s) that you want to hide. On the Ribbon's Home tab, choose Format⇨Hide & Unhide⇨Hide Columns, or choose Format⇨Hide & Unhide⇨Hide Rows.

- Select the column or row header(s) you want to hide. *See* "Selecting entire rows and columns," in Part 4. On the Ribbon's Home tab, choose Format⇨Hide & Unhide⇨Hide Columns, or choose Format⇨Hide & Unhide⇨Hide Rows. Alternatively, right-click the selected row or column header(s) and choose Hide from the contextual menu.

- Drag a column header's right border all the way to the left or a row header's bottom border all the way upward.

Remember: A hidden column or row has a width or height of 0. If you use the arrow keys to move the active cell pointer, you skip cells in hidden columns or rows. In other words, you can't use the arrow keys to move to a cell in a hidden row or column.

See also the next section, "Unhiding columns and rows."

Unhiding columns and rows

Unhiding a hidden row or column can prove a bit tricky because you can't directly select a row or column that's hidden.

To unhide one or more column(s) or row(s), choose one of the following options:

- Select any cells on the worksheets on either side of the column(s) or row(s) that you want to unhide. In Figure 8-7, for example, if you want to unhide columns E and F, select any row on the worksheet and select cells in columns D and G. On the Ribbon's Home tab, choose Format⇨Hide & Unhide⇨Unhide Columns, or choose Format⇨Hide & Unhide⇨Unhide Rows.

- Select the column or row header(s) on either side of the row(s) or column(s) you want to unhide. *See* "Selecting entire rows and columns," in Part 4. On the Ribbon's Home tab, choose Format⇨Hide & Unhide⇨Unhide Columns, or choose Format⇨Hide & Unhide⇨Unhide Rows. Alternatively, right-click the selected row or column header(s) and choose Unhide from the contextual menu.

Figure 8-7

	A	B	C	D	G	H
1	Commission Rate	3.50%		Normal commission rate		
2	Sales Goal	15%		Improvement from prior month		
3	Bonus Rate	2%		Paid if individual sales goal is attained		
4						
5	Sales Rep	Last Month	This Month	Change	Commission	
6	Alan Devonshare	$ 187,464	$ 237,057	$ 49,593	$ 13,038	
7	Devon Kendricks	$ 235,407	$ 283,066	$ 47,659	$ 15,569	
8	Candice Wilkenson	$ 209,992	$ 158,597	$ (51,395)	$ 5,551	
9	Wayne Clarke	$ 135,073	$ 127,898	$ (7,175)	$ 4,476	
10	Roger Mitchell	$ 144,568	$ 166,356	$ 21,788	$ 9,150	
11	Jennifer Walker	$ 140,932	$ 141,048	$ 116	$ 4,937	
12	Total	1053436	1114022		$ 52,720	
13						

TIP

To unhide all hidden columns or rows, select the entire worksheet (by pressing Ctrl+A or clicking the blank box that intersects the row and column headings). Then choose Format⇨Hide & Unhide⇨Unhide Columns, or choose Format⇨Hide & Unhide⇨Unhide Rows

Modifying Cell Size

You may want to change the width of a column if it's not wide enough to display values (indicated when the column displays a series of pound signs — #######) or to simply space out the cells horizontally. Changing the row height is useful for spacing out rows and is sometimes better than inserting empty rows between rows of data.

Changing column width

To change the width of one or more columns, choose one of the following options:

✔ Select any cell(s) on the worksheets in the column(s) that you want to adjust. On the Ribbon's Home tab, click the Format button, choose Width from the menu, and enter a value in the Column Width dialog box that appears. Alternatively, choose AutoFit Selection from the menu. This command adjusts the width of the selected column(s) so that the widest entry in the column fits.

✔ Drag the right border of the column heading with the mouse until the column is the width that you want. As you drag, Excel displays a ScreenTip that shows the current column width (see Figure 8-8). If you select multiple column headers and drag the right border of any one of the column headers, all columns adjust accordingly.

Figure 8-8

(spreadsheet figure showing columns A, B, C, D with "F13" cell reference and "Width: 9.29 (70 pixels)" tooltip; column B rows 1–3 show ########)

✔ Double-click the right border of a column heading to automatically set the column width to the widest entry in the column. If you select multiple column headers and double-click the right border of any one of the column headers, each column width is set automatically to the widest entry in the column.

✔ Select the column heading(s) of the column(s) you want to adjust. Right-click the column header(s), choose Column Width from the contextual menu, and enter a value in the Column Width dialog box that appears.

TIP To change the default width of all columns, click the Format button and choose Default Width from the menu. This command opens the Standard Width dialog box, in which you enter the new default column width. All columns that weren't previously adjusted take on the new column width.

Changing row height

You measure row height in *points* (a standard unit of measurement in the printing trade; 72 points equal 1 inch). To change the height of one or more rows, choose one of the following options:

✔ Select any cell(s) on the worksheets in the row(s) that you want to adjust. On the Ribbon's Home tab, click the Format button, choose Height from the menu, and enter a value in the Row Height dialog box that appears.

✔ Drag the bottom border of the row heading with the mouse until the row is the height that you want. As you drag, Excel displays a ScreenTip that shows the current row height. If you select multiple row headers and drag the bottom border of any one of the row headers, all rows adjust accordingly.

✔ Select the row heading(s) of the row(s) that you want to adjust. Right-click the row header(s), choose Row Height from the contextual menu, and enter a value in the Row Height dialog box that appears.

Remember: Excel adjusts the row height automatically to accommodate the tallest entry in the row.

Using Cell Styles

If you find yourself continuously applying the same combination of fonts, lines, shading, number format, and so on to cells or ranges in your worksheet, using cell styles instead will save you time.

Excel provides a Cell Styles gallery with several predefined styles (see Figure 8-9.) You can modify a predefined style or create a new style from scratch. The Cell Styles gallery includes Titles and Headings styles and Themed Cell Styles categories that change if you change the workbook theme. The default font used for styles in the other predefined categories in the gallery matches the body font of the selected theme and therefore changes as the theme changes. *See also* "Formatting with Themes," in Part 1.

Figure 8-9

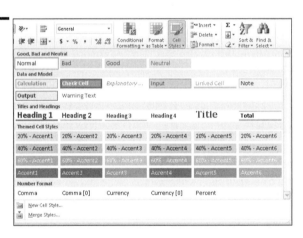

A cell style can include any combination of the following formatting elements:

- ✔ Number format
- ✔ Font (type, size, and color)
- ✔ Alignment (vertical and horizontal)
- ✔ Border
- ✔ Pattern
- ✔ Protection (locked and hidden)

Applying a predefined cell style

Follow these steps to apply a predefined style:

1. Select the cell or range to which you want to apply the style. You can select a contiguous or noncontiguous range. ***See also*** "Selecting Cells and Ranges," in Part 4.

2. Click the Cell Styles button on the Ribbon's Home tab. Excel displays a gallery of predefined styles.

3. Choose a style from the gallery to immediately apply the style. If you hover the mouse pointer over a style, Excel provides a preview of the style in your selected cell or range. The style is not applied until you click it.

The Cells Styles gallery includes a few categories with styles that you can use as a guide for representing certain types of data. For example, you can use the Good, Bad, and Neutral styles to highlight data in your worksheet that's considered good, bad, or neutral. You can use the Data and Model styles to represent input cells, cells that involve calculations (formulas), and so on. These two style categories use a theme font and non-theme colors. If you select a new theme for the workbook, the font changes to match the new theme but the colors remain unchanged.

Select a style from the Themed Cell style category if you want to format a range to match other elements on the worksheet that use theme styles (a chart, for example). If you change the theme applied to the workbook, the formatting of the range changes to match the new theme.

See also "Formatting with Themes," in Part 1.

Modifying an existing style

The Cell Styles gallery is an example of the Ribbon's *results-oriented* approach, providing predefined layouts that you're likely to be satisfied with. However, if none of the available styles are exactly what you want but are close, you can simply modify an existing style rather than create a new style from scratch. For example, you might be happy with a certain style's font and background color but not the number format, or you might like the number format and font but not the background color.

Follow these steps to modify an existing style:

1. Click the Cell Styles button on the Ribbon's Home tab, right-click a style, and choose Modify from the menu that appears. Excel displays the Style dialog box.

2. If you want, type a new name for the style in the Style Name box.

3. In the Style Includes section, click to add or clear a check mark next to the formatting elements you want to include or not include in the modified style.

4. Click the Format button. Excel displays the Format Cells dialog box.

5. Select the appropriate tabs and formatting options you want.

6. Click OK to exit the Format Cells dialog box and click OK again to close the Style dialog box. Excel updates the style in the gallery with the changes you made.

Creating a custom cell style

If none of the styles available in the Cell Styles gallery meet your needs either directly or by modifying a style, you can create a style from scratch. Follow these steps to create a custom cell style:

1. Click the Cell Styles button on the Ribbon's Home tab, and then choose New Cell Style (at the bottom of the gallery). Excel displays the Style dialog box.

2. In the Style Name box, type a name for the style.

3. Complete Steps 3 to 6 in the section "Modifying an existing style," immediately preceding this section. Excel adds the style to a new Custom category section it creates in the Cell Styles gallery.

Copying (merging) cell styles from another workbook

If you modify existing styles or create several custom styles in a workbook, you may want these styles to appear in other workbooks. Merging styles from another workbook can save a lot of time because you don't have to recreate the styles manually in every new workbook in which you want to use the styles.

Follow these steps to merge a style from another workbook:

1. Ensure that the workbook from which you want to merge the styles is open.

2. Activate the workbook you want to merge the styles to.

3. Click the Cell Styles button on the Ribbon's Home tab, and then choose Merge Styles (at the bottom of the gallery). Excel displays the Merge Styles dialog box.

4. In the Merge Styles From list box, select the workbook from which you will be merging the styles and click OK.

5. Excel asks you to confirm whether you want to merge styles with the same names as styles in the workbook that you're merging to. In most cases, you want to click No. Excel merges the styles into the active workbook.

6. To view the merged styles, click the Cell Styles button.

Previewing and Printing Your Work

Many worksheets that you develop with Excel are designed to serve as printed reports. Printing from Excel is easy, and you can generate attractive reports with minimal effort. Excel offers numerous printing options, which we explain in this part.

In this part . . .

- ✔ Adjusting Page and Printer Settings
- ✔ Changing the Worksheet Display Mode
- ✔ Inserting a Header or Footer
- ✔ Setting the Print Area

Adjusting Page and Printer Settings

Excel 2010 consolidates page and printer settings on the Print tab in the Backstage view. *See also* "Going Backstage," in Part 1. Figure 9-1 shows the options on the Print tab. Most of these options include brief explanatory text or are otherwise self-explanatory.

Setting page and printer options

Click the File tab on the Ribbon to enter the Backstage view. Then click the Print tab. Use the following options on the Print tab to adjust printer settings. Note that if your printer doesn't support a specific feature, the option won't appear in the tab. (For example, if your printer doesn't support double-sided printing, you won't see that option.) Therefore, the list you see will be different depending on the capabilities of your printer:

- **Copies:** Use the Copies spinner control to specify the number of copies you want to print.

- **Printer:** The printer drop-down gallery button displays the current printer selection. Click the button and choose another printer, if required.

- **Printer Properties:** Click the Printer Properties link below the printer drop-down gallery button to display and modify properties for the selected printer.

- **Print range:** By default, this drop-down gallery button displays Print Active Sheets. Click the button to select a different option from the galley menu.

  Normally, if you have print areas set for one or more worksheets, Excel prints only the print area range or ranges (data outside the print area is not printed). If you want to override the print area settings, select the Ignore Print Area option at the bottom of the gallery menu. Excel places a check mark next to the option to indicate that it's set. Select the option again to clear the setting. *See also* "Setting the Print Area," later in this part.

- **Pages:** Use the Pages spinner controls to specify the range of pages you want to print.

- **One- or two-sided printing:** By default, this drop-down gallery button displays Print One Sided. Click the button to select a two-sided option, if required.

- **Collation:** By default, this drop-down gallery button displays the Collated option. Click the button to select the Uncollated option, if required.

- **Page orientation:** By default, this drop-down gallery button displays Portrait Orientation. Click the button to select Landscape Orientation, if required.

✔ **Page size:** By default, this drop-down gallery button displays the Letter option. Click the button to select a different size option from the galley menu.

If the size you want isn't listed, choose More Paper Sizes at the bottom of the gallery menu. In the dialog box that appears, choose a size from the Page Size drop-down list.

✔ **Margins:** By default, this drop-down gallery button displays the Normal Margins option. Click the button to select a different option from the galley menu.

If you need finer control over the margin settings, or if you want to center your printed output, choose Custom Margins at the bottom of the gallery menu. Excel displays the Page Setup dialog box with the Margins tab selected. Use the spinner controls to change the margin values and the check boxes for centering the output on the page.

✔ **Scaling:** By default, this drop-down gallery button displays No Scaling. Click the button to select a different scaling option from the galley menu.

If you need finer control over scaling, choose Custom Scaling Options at the bottom of the gallery menu. Excel displays the Page Setup dialog box with the Page tab selected. Make your adjustments in the Scaling section of the tab.

Previewing your pages

The Print tab includes a convenient Print Preview area, as shown in Figure 9-1. Navigate between successive pages by using the arrows at the bottom-left of this area, or go directly to a specific page by entering a page number in the Current Page box and pressing Enter.

At the bottom-right of the Print Preview area are the Show Margins and Zoom to Page buttons. Click the Show Margins button to toggle on and off the display of margin lines. When the margin lines are displayed, you can adjust the margins by dragging the lines with the mouse. There are two sets of horizontal margin lines. One set controls header and top page margins, and the other set controls the footer and bottom page margins for the print range.

Click the Zoom to Page button to toggle between zooming out to see an entire page and zooming in for a closer look at the page contents. You may not see much difference between the two zoom modes, depending on the page size and screen resolution. When you zoom out, you can use the scroll bar to scroll through all the pages that you will be printing. When you zoom in, the scroll bar allows you to see more of a page — if you set a sufficiently large page size, or have relatively low screen resolution, or both.

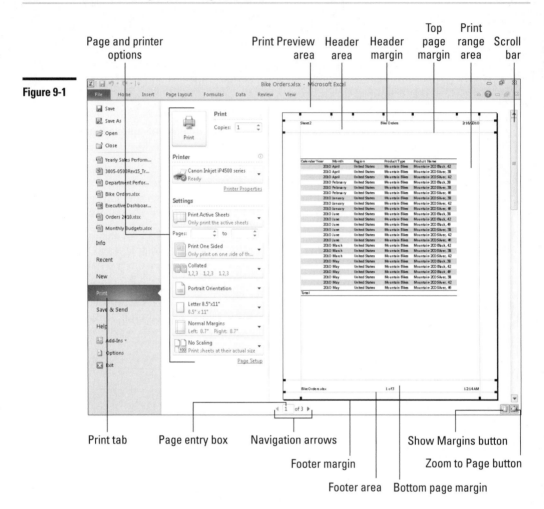

Figure 9-1

Changing the Worksheet Display Mode

Excel provides the following two special worksheet display modes that you can work in with documents that you intend to print:

- **Page break preview:** This display mode shows a bird's-eye view of your worksheet with lines indicating the location of page breaks and page number watermarks identifying the pages. This display mode is useful for setting or adjusting manual page breaks.

✔ **Page layout view:** The new page layout view shows your work in the context of the printed page (see Figure 9-2). This display mode has the following characteristics:

- It shows individual pages with headers and footers, margins, page orientation, and common worksheet print settings (such as row and column headers or row and column data labels if selected).

- The view is fully editable, so that you can use this mode in lieu of the normal display mode for any document you intend to print. Note, however, that you will see less data on-screen than in the normal display mode.

- Pages that will not print are shaded and contain the phrase *Click to add data* watermark.

You can switch between display modes easily by clicking a display mode button on the right side of the status bar (see Figure 9-2) or by clicking a mode button on the Ribbon's View tab.

Handling Page Breaks

If you print multiple-page reports, you know that controlling page breaks is often important. You normally don't want a row to print on a page by itself, for example. Excel handles page breaks automatically. After you print or preview your worksheet, Excel displays dashed lines on the worksheet in normal display mode to indicate where page breaks occur. Sometimes, you want to force a page break — either a vertical or a horizontal one. If your worksheet consists of several distinct areas, for example, you may want to print each area on a separate sheet of paper.

Inserting manual page breaks

To override Excel's automatic handling of page breaks, you must manually insert one or more page breaks. To insert a horizontal page break, follow these steps:

1. Move the cell pointer to the row where you want to begin the new page, but make sure that the cell pointer is in column A. (Otherwise, you insert a vertical page break *and* a horizontal page break.)

2. Click the Page Layout tab on the Ribbon, click the Page Break button, and choose Insert Page Break from the menu. Excel inserts the page break in the row that is above the cell pointer.

Top
margin
area

Left
margin
area

Left
header
area

Ruler

Center
header
area

Right
header
area

Right
margin
area

Figure 9-2

Ruler

Normal view

Page layout view

Page break preview

Nonprinting
page

To insert a vertical page break, follow these steps:

1. Move the cell pointer to the column where you want to begin the new page, but make sure that the cell pointer is in row 1. (Otherwise, you insert a horizontal page break *and* a vertical page break).

2. Click the Page Layout tab on the Ribbon, click the Breaks button, and choose Insert Page Break from the menu. Excel inserts the page break in the column to the left of the cell pointer.

TIP

You can often get a better perspective of where to insert breaks in your worksheet by creating your page breaks in the page break preview display mode. *See* "Previewing and adjusting page breaks," later in this section.

Removing manual page breaks

To remove a manual page break, follow these steps:

1. Move the cell pointer anywhere in the first row *below* a horizontal page break or in the first column to the *right* of a vertical page break.

2. Click the Page Layout tab on the Ribbon, click the Breaks button, and choose Remove Page Break from the menu.

To remove all manual page breaks in the worksheet, click the Page Layout tab on the Ribbon, click the Breaks button, and choose Reset All Page Breaks from the menu.

Previewing and adjusting page breaks

Click the Page Break Preview button on the right side of the status bar or click the Page Break Preview button on the Ribbon's View tab to enter the page break preview mode. This mode displays your worksheet in a way that enables you to move the page breaks by dragging them with your mouse (see Figure 9-3). This view doesn't show a true page preview. (For example, it doesn't show headers and footers.) But it's an easy way to make sure that the pages break at desired locations.

Figure 9-3

Remember the following points as you use the page break preview mode:

✔ Excel automatically zooms out so that you can see more on-screen. You can set the zoom factor to any value that you want by using the zoom controls on the status bar.

✔ If you specify a print area (rather than the entire worksheet), the print area appears in white and all the other cells appear in a darker color.

✔ You can adjust a page break by dragging the line that identifies a break location.

✔ In this display mode, Excel shows manual page breaks as solid lines and automatic breaks as dashed lines.

✔ While you're previewing the page breaks, you have full access to all Excel commands.

Remember: If you increase the amount of information to be printed on a page having a manual break, Excel automatically scales the output to fit the page.

Inserting a Header or Footer

A *header* is information that appears at the top of each printed page. A *footer* is information that appears at the bottom of each printed page.

Headers and footers each have three sections: left, center, and right. You can, for example, specify a header that consists of your name left-justified, the worksheet name centered, and the page number right-justified.

The easiest way to include a header or footer in your printouts is to add the header or footer in the header and footer regions of the page layout view mode (see Figure 9-4). Either click the Page Layout View button, on the right side of the status bar, or click the Page Layout View button on the Ribbon's View tab to enter the page layout view mode.

The header and footer regions in the page layout view have the following characteristics:

✔ The regions appear immediately above and below the worksheet data area.

✔ If the header or footer regions are empty, the center section of each region includes a watermark. The header watermark is labeled *Click to add header* and the footer watermark is labeled *Click to add footer.*

✔ If you hover the mouse pointer over a header or footer section, Excel shades the section to indicate the area that the section covers. Simply click in a section to add information.

✔ By default, the same header and footer appears on each page.

✔ Excel displays the information in the header or footer area as it would appear on the printed page.

Figure 9-4

Remember: By default, Excel doesn't automatically include a header or footer in your printouts if you don't specify any information to include in the header or footer.

Selecting a predefined header or footer

To select a predefined header or footer, follow these steps:

1. Select the Page Layout View by clicking the Page Layout View button on the status bar or on the Ribbon's View tab.

2. Click in a section of the header or footer region. The Ribbon displays the Header & Footer Tools contextual tab header on Excel's title bar and the Design tab below the header.

3. If necessary, click the Design tab to display the header/footer tools on the Ribbon.

4. Click the Header or Footer button and choose an option from the menu.

5. Click anywhere in the worksheet to remove the display of the header/footer tools on the Ribbon. Excel inserts the selected header or footer in the page.

Remember: You can insert the header/footer information in any page of your document and Excel will automatically apply the header/footer to all other pages. **See also** "Using multiple headers and footers in your reports," later in this section.

Creating a custom header or footer

To define a custom header or footer, follow these steps:

1. Complete Steps 1 to 3 in "Selecting a predefined header or footer," immediately preceding in this section.

2. Enter the desired information in any or all of the three sections of the header or footer; or click any of the eight buttons in the Header and Footer Elements group (described in the following table) to enter a special code.

Button	Code	Function
Page Number	&[Page]	Inserts the page number
Number of Pages	&[Pages]	Inserts the total number of pages to print
Current Date	&[Date]	Inserts the current date
Current Time	&[Time]	Inserts the current time
File Path	&[Path]&[File]	Inserts the path and filename of the workbook
File Name	&[File]	Inserts the workbook's name
Sheet Name	&[Tab]	Inserts the sheet's name
Picture	&[Picture]	Enables you to choose a picture to insert in the header or footer

After you click away from the section in which you added a code, Excel converts the code to the information that will appear on the printed page.

3. If you need to format the header or footer text, click the Ribbon's Home tab and select from the available tools in the Font group.

4. Click anywhere in the worksheet to remove the display of the header/footer tools on the Ribbon.

The Format Picture button in the Header and Footer Elements group is available only if you insert a picture in the header or footer. Clicking this button displays the Format Picture dialog box, where you can select options to size, rotate, scale, crop, and adjust the picture.

 TIP You can combine text and codes and insert as many codes as you want into each section. If the text that you enter uses an ampersand (&), you must enter it twice (because Excel uses an ampersand to signal a code). For example, to enter the text *Research & Development* into a header or footer, type *Research && Development.*

You can use as many lines as you want in your header or footer section. You may have to adjust the top or bottom margin, however, to prevent the header or footer from spilling into the worksheet area. Position the mouse pointer where you want to add another line or wrap an existing line, and press Enter.

Remember: You insert the header or footer information on any page of your document and Excel automatically applies the header or footer to all other pages. *See also* "Using multiple headers and footers in your reports," immediately following this section.

Using multiple headers and footers in your reports

Excel provides the following options when specifying headers and footers for different pages in your reports:

- ✔ You can specify a different header or footer for the first page. This option is useful, for example, for reports that require a different header or footer for a title or table of contents page.

- ✔ You can specify a different header or footer for odd and even pages. This option is useful, for example, if you create book-style reports. If, in addition, you specify a first page header or footer, Excel applies the odd page header or footer starting from the second page of your report.

Follow these steps to add a separate header or footer to the first page or to add separate headers or footers to odd and even pages of your report:

1. Complete Steps 1 to 3 in "Selecting a predefined header or footer," earlier in this section.

2. Do one or both of the following:

- To specify a first page header or footer, select the Different First Page check box in the Options group of the Header and Footer Design tab.

- To specify odd and even page headers or footers, select the Different Odd & Even Pages check box in the Options group of the Header and Footer Design tab.

3. Enter the header or footer information for each page as follows:

- If you specified a separate first page header or footer only, enter the first page header or footer information in the first page of your document and enter the header or footer information for all subsequent pages in the second page of your document.

- If you specified odd and even headers or footers only, enter the header or footer information for all odd pages in the first page of your document and enter the header or footer information for all even pages in the second page of your document.

- If you specified both first page header or footer and odd and even page headers or footers, enter the first page header or footer information in the first page of your document, enter the header or footer information for all odd pages in the second page of your document, and enter the header or footer information for all even pages in the third page of your document.

Remember: When you click the mouse pointer within a header or footer region, Excel indicates the type of header or footer you're working with (normal, first page, odd page, or even page) above the header or below the footer area.

Setting the Print Area

If you choose to print the active worksheet or multiple sheets, Excel prints the entire sheet or sheets — or just the range named Print_Area. Each worksheet can have a range named Print_Area. After you set the print area, Excel automatically creates the Print_Area name. Print_Area is a standard named range, so you can edit the range's reference manually if you like. *See also* "Editing Names," in Part 6.

To set the print area, follow these steps:

1. Select the range that you want to print. Press and hold Ctrl to select non-adjacent ranges.

2. Click the Page Layout tab on the Ribbon, click the Print Area button, and choose Set Print Area from the menu.

Remember: After you specify a print area, by default Excel uses that print area in all subsequent printouts. If you want to clear the print area (so that Excel automatically prints the entire worksheet,) click the Print Area button and choose Clear Print Area from the menu.

If you don't want to clear the normal print areas that you create but occasionally want to ignore the print areas (to print the entire worksheet), select the Ignore Print Area option from the Print Range button menu in the Backstage view. *See* "Setting page and printer options," earlier in this part.

Specifying Sheet Printing Options

In most cases, you want to print the worksheet as displayed on-screen. Sometimes, however, you may want to control how or what elements are printed. Excel provides several options that allow you to control the appearance of your worksheet printouts.

Printing gridlines or row and column headings

Follow these steps to control the printing of gridlines or row and column headings:

1. Click the Page Layout tab on the Ribbon.

2. Do one or both of the following:

   • To print or suppress printing of gridlines, select or deselect the Print check box under the Gridlines heading in the Sheet Options group.

   • To print or suppress printing of row and column headings, select or deselect the Print check box under the Headings heading in the Sheet Options group.

Printing row or column data labels on each page

Worksheet data is often set up with labels (titles) in the first row and sometimes descriptive names in the first column. If such a worksheet requires more than one page to print, you may find reading subsequent pages difficult because the text in the first row or the first column or both doesn't print on subsequent pages. Excel offers an option that allows you to print row and column labels (titles) on every page.

Follow these steps to select the row or column labels that will appear on each page:

1. Click the Page Layout tab on the Ribbon and then click the Print Titles button. Excel displays the Page Setup dialog box with the Sheet tab selected.

2. Click inside the appropriate box in the Print Titles area, and point to the row(s) or column(s) in the worksheet that you want to repeat on each page. You can also enter these references manually. For example, to spec-ify rows 1 and 2 as repeating rows, enter **1:2**.

3. Click OK to close the Page Setup dialog box.

Remember: Don't confuse print titles with headers; these are two different con-cepts. Headers appear at the top of each page and contain information such as the worksheet name, date, or page number. Print titles describe the data that you're printing, such as field names in a table.

You can specify different print titles for each worksheet in the workbook. Excel remembers print titles by creating sheet-level names (Print_Titles).

Selecting miscellaneous sheet printing options

Excel provides some worksheet print options that you might use occasionally. Follow these steps to access these options:

1. Click the Page Layout tab on the Ribbon and then click the dialog launcher button on the bottom right of the Sheet Options group container, or frame. *See* "Introducing the Ribbon," in Part 1 for a discussion of the dialog launcher. Excel displays the Page Setup dialog box with the Sheet tab selected.

2. Select among these options:

    *   **Black and White:** If you have a colorful worksheet but your printer is stuck in a monochrome world, you may discover that the worksheet colors don't translate well to black and white. In this case, you can use this option to instruct Excel to ignore the colors while printing.

    *   **Draft Quality:** Printing in Draft mode doesn't print embedded charts or drawing objects, cell gridlines, or borders. This mode usually reduces the printing time and is handy for getting a quick printout.

    *   **Comments:** If one or more cells in your worksheet have a cell comment, you can print these comments along with the worksheet by choosing an option from the Comments drop-down list. By default, comments are not printed.

    *   **Cell Errors As:** Excel gives you the option to print error values as they appear on your worksheet or to replace each error value with a pre-defined character in the printed output. Error values are #NUM!, #DIV/0!, #REF!, #N/A, #VALUE!, #NAME?, and #NULL!. Choose an option from the Cell Errors As drop-down list. By default, errors are printed as displayed.

    *   **Page Order:** If you have a worksheet that spans across several columns and down several rows, your worksheet is likely to end up with multiple vertical page breaks, horizontal page breaks, or both. In this case, you have the choice of printing your worksheet pages from left to right or from top to bottom. In the Page Order area, click the Down, Then Over option or the Over, Then Down option. By default, Excel prints down, then over.

3. Click OK to close the Page Setup dialog box.

Charting Your Data

A chart (also known as a *graph* outside Excel circles) is a way to present a table of numbers visually. The visual display allows you, for example, to quickly examine trends, patterns, anomalies, or compare the relative contributions of various items. Excel provides you with the tools to create a variety of charts.

In this part . . .

- ✔ Adding a New Data Series to a Chart
- ✔ Adding Context to Numbers with Sparklines
- ✔ Changing the Chart Type for an Existing Chart or Data Series
- ✔ Creating and Adding Elements to a Chart
- ✔ Formatting a Chart Element
- ✔ Modifying a Chart Axis

Anatomy of a Chart

Before you create your first chart in Excel, it helps to know the elements that you can include in the chart. Figure 10-1 illustrates the most common elements that a chart can contain. When you create a chart, include only the elements you need to clearly portray your data. Too much information will make the chart hard to read and reduce its usefulness.

Figure 10-1

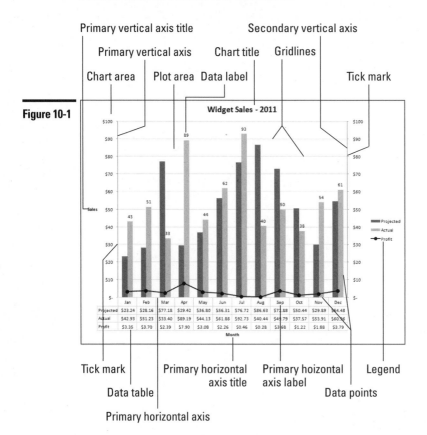

The following is a description of the elements shown in Figure 10-1:

- ✔ **Horizontal axis:** For most charts, this axis displays category labels. A *category* is any item without numerical significance. Month, Quarter, and Product are examples of categories. For a Month category, the labels might be Jan, Feb, Mar, and so on. The chart displays the labels at equally spaced intervals on the axis. For the bar, X Y scatter, and bubble chart types, the horizontal axis displays a value scale. A chart can have a *primary* horizontal axis and a *secondary* horizontal axis (not shown in Figure 10-1).

- ✔ **Horizontal axis title:** Displays a name for the category plotted.

- ✔ **Vertical axis:** For most charts, this axis displays a value scale for the data series plotted. For the bar chart type, the vertical axis displays category labels. A chart can have a *primary* and a *secondary* vertical axis.

- ✔ **Vertical axis title:** Displays a name for the value scale against which the series is plotted.

- ✔ **Data series:** A group of values (data points) associated with a category. For example, projected sales and actual sales might be two series associated with a Month category.

- ✔ **Data points:** Values associated with category labels. For example, projected and actual sales figures plotted for January represent data points.

- ✔ **Data labels:** Labels associated with the data points on the chart. For example, the labels can be the values of data points.

- ✔ **Data table:** The data series represented in tabular form and placed directly below the horizontal axis.

- ✔ **Chart title:** A title that you provide for the chart.

- ✔ **Legend:** A group of keys and text identifying each data series in the chart.

- ✔ **Gridlines:** Lines placed on the chart to assist in reading the value of data points or to segregate category labels. Gridlines can be distracting and therefore should be used sparingly. If you must use gridlines, we suggest that you choose a pale and unobtrusive color for the line.

- ✔ **Tick marks:** These short lines mark off intervals on an axis.

- ✔ **Plot area:** The area of the chart, defined by the axes boundaries, where the data series is plotted.

- ✔ **Chart area:** The entire area that includes all elements within the chart.

Activating a Chart

Before you can do anything with a chart, you must activate it, as follows:

- ✔ To activate a chart on a chart sheet, click the chart sheet's tab.

- ✔ To activate a chart that you embed in a worksheet, click the chart border area.

After you activate an embedded chart or a chart on a chart sheet, Excel displays the Chart Tools contextual tabs on the Ribbon. Double-clicking the chart automatically displays the Design tab tools on the Ribbon.

Adding Context to Numbers with Sparklines

A *sparkline* is a miniature chart that occupies a single worksheet cell. Sparklines are not intended to show the detail you would typically see on a standard Excel chart. Instead, they serve as at-a-glance graphical displays to help add context to numbers.

In Figure 10-2, we see that the most recent values of product sales are in the 31-Jan-11 column. The line-type sparklines show the 12-month trend of sales for the product categories, and the column-type sparklines show individual values over the same period.

Figure 10-2

	A	B	C	D	E	F	G	H	I	J	K	L
1	Products	12-Month Trend	Monthly Comparison	31-Jan-11	31-Dec-10	30-Nov-10	31-Oct-10	30-Sep-10	31-Aug-10	31-Jul-10	30-Jun-10	31-May-10	30-
2	Product1			283	404	378	207	493	249	341	326	497
3	Product2			269	343	303	403	468	431	365	334	212
4	Product3			382	228	494	406	290	223	299	248	278
5	Product4			319	487	284	500	498	320	500	457	233
6	Product5			289	209	370	297	297	242	457	446	234
7	Product6			372	278	305	425	209	425	420	211	364
8	Product7			370	375	282	322	407	222	460	487	315
9	Product8			464	357	433	423	299	220	391	456	440
10	Product9			385	444	429	230	415	454	226	468	333
11	Product10			371	461	423	434	449	206	319	446	427
12	Product11			423	460	214	233	312	317	480	341	350
13	Product12			357	294	222	328	413	370	367	235	282
14	Product13			311	271	276	439	495	297	285	496	476
15	Product14			285	261	482	276	224	456	255	316	353
16	Product15			397	238	380	407	441	386	220	213	224
17	Product16			273	305	409	364	443	307	417	293	459
18	Product17			242	442	209	312	456	296	471	349	386
19	Product18			483	258	229	401	330	414	204	475	245
20	Product19			405	247	260	233	450	495	403	487	484
21	Product20			361	258	455	409	438	383	488	219	385
22	Product21			375	251	286	383	307	398	374	357	251
23	Product22			348	375	486	373	259	267	366	225	240
24	Product23			263	263	432	286	211	339	328	312	250
25	Total			8027	7509	7991	8091	8604	7719	8436	8197	7718
26												

Sparklines are useful in a *dashboard* display. In a typical dashboard, you would show only the current value and an associated sparkline for historical context. A dashboard that includes the product sales of Figure 10-2, for example, might show the top five or ten products for Jan-11 along with 12-month line-type sparklines.

Remember: You cannot select a sparkline in a cell the way you can select, for example, text in a cell. In this section, when we refer to selecting a sparkline, we really mean selecting the cell or range containing the sparkline or sparklines.

Creating a sparkline

Follow these steps to create a sparkline:

1. Click the Insert tab on the Ribbon and select one of the following sparkline types: Line, Column, and Win/Loss. Excel displays the Create Sparkline dialog box.

TIP

If you want to create sparklines in a worksheet different from the worksheet holding the data range for the sparklines, start this step in the worksheet that will hold the sparklines.

2. Click in the Data Range box and enter the data range for the sparkline(s). You can enter the range manually or use the mouse to select the range in the worksheet.

   • To create a single sparkline, select data in a single row or single column.

   • To create multiple sparklines, select more than one row and column.

3. Click in the Location Range box. If Excel selects a location range and it's not what you want, clear the entry.

   • If you selected a single row or column in Step 2, enter a single cell for the sparkline.

   • If you selected more than one row and column in Step 2, select a range for the sparklines. The range must be in a single row or a single column. The number of cells in the range must be equal to the numbers of rows in the data range or the number of columns in the data range. If the number of cells in the range is equal to the number of data rows, the sparklines in the group will be created from data in the rows. If the number of cells in the range is equal to the number of data columns, the sparklines in the group will be created from data in the columns. If the number of cells in the range is not equal to the number of rows or columns in the data range, Excel displays an error.

   In Figure 10-2, we selected a column range for the sparklines, and the number of cells in the range is equal to the number of data rows. Therefore, for each sparkline, Excel used the data in each row.

4. After you specify the sparkline location range, click OK.

When you select a sparkline, Excel displays the Sparkline Tools Design tab on the Ribbon.

Grouping and ungrouping sparklines

After you create multiple sparklines using the Create Sparkline dialog box, Excel places the resulting sparklines in a *group*. If you click any sparkline in the group, Excel displays a blue highlight surrounding the group. The purpose of the group is to allow you to apply settings, such as formatting changes, to all the sparklines in the group simultaneously.

If you want to remove one or more sparklines from the group, you can do so in two ways:

✔ Select the sparklines that you want to ungroup. Click the Sparkline Tools Design tab on the Ribbon and click the Ungroup button.

✔ Select the sparklines that you want to ungroup. Right-click any of the selected sparklines and choose Sparklines⇨Ungroup from the menu.

In Figure 10-2, I created a sparkline group that includes a Total row. For comparison among product sales sparklines, I set the vertical axis minimum and maximum values the same for all sparklines. (*See* "Using Sparkline axis options," later in this section.) Because the values in the totals data range is an order of magnitude higher than the individual product values, the sparklines for the totals would not have shown the variations in its data values adequately. I therefore ungrouped the sparklines for the Total row.

To group sparklines, simply select the sparklines you want to group and click the Group button in the Sparkline Tools Design tab.

Modifying a sparkline data range or location

After you create a sparkline, you can change its data range or location. Select the sparkline and click the Sparkline Tools Design tab on the Ribbon.

On the far left of the Design tab is the Sparkline group, which contains a single button called Edit Data. Clicking the button's arrow displays a menu that allows you to

✔ Change the source or location range for a sparkline group.

✔ Change the source range for an individual sparkline.

✔ Tell Excel how you want to handle hidden or missing data in the sparkline data range.

✔ Switch the data range used by sparklines in a group from rows to columns or vice versa. When you create a sparkline group, if the number of data rows and data columns are the same, by default each sparkline in the group is created from data in the rows. You can use the Switch Row/ Column option to force the sparklines in the group to use data in the columns instead.

TIP You can move a sparkline or a sparkline group to another location by selecting and dragging, or by a cut-and-paste operation. The procedure is similar to moving a worksheet range. *See* "Moving Cells and Ranges," in Part 4.

Including additional elements in your sparkline

Excel allows you to add additional elements to a sparkline. Select the sparkline and click the Sparkline Tools Design tab on the Ribbon. Then select the elements you want to include by clicking the appropriate check boxes in the Show/Hide group. Note that the Markers option applies only to line-type sparklines.

Formatting and changing the sparkline type

You can change the color of your sparkline and any added elements, and you change the sparkline type. Select the sparkline and click the Sparkline Tools Design tab on the Ribbon.

The Type group allows you to change the type of sparkline. The choices are Line, Column, and Win/Loss.

In the Style group, you can select predefined color styles from the gallery. Any highlight element that you turn on in the Show/Hide group appears with predefined colors in the Styles group.

If none of the predefined styles are to your liking, you can select a sparkline color or weight (or both in the case of a line sparkline) from the Sparkline Color menu. You can select the color of various highlight elements by choosing a color from the Marker Color menu.

Using sparkline axis options

As in a standard Excel chart, sparklines have horizontal and vertical axes, but they are normally hidden. Excel provides several axis options that you can use with sparklines. Select a sparkline, click the Sparkline Tools Design tab, and then click the Axis button to display the following list of options for the sparkline horizontal and vertical axes, respectively:

✓ **Horizontal axis options:** These options allow you to change the default behavior of the horizontal axis.

- By default, Excel uses the General Axis Type. This is equivalent to the category axis in a standard Excel chart. Note that all sparklines in a group share a *single* horizontal axis. You don't actually select a range for the general horizontal axis type; the axis is inferred from the data range. In Figure 10-2, the column labels in the data range are actual dates (not just month or year labels), so they can be used as a horizontal axis. Choose Date Axis Type from the menu, click in the dialog box that appears, and select the date labels. The difference between the general axis and the date axis is as follows: If in Figure 10-2, one or more of the month columns were missing, the date axis would show the missing months as gaps in the sparkline. With the general axis, there would be no gaps in the sparkline.

- You can display the horizontal axis in the sparkline by choosing Show Axis from the menu. The axis is displayed only if at least one negative value is in a sparkline data range. The axis is therefore useful for showing the zero crossing point in a line-type sparkline.

- By default, when you select a data range for a sparkline, Excel plots the data from left to right or top to bottom. If you want to plot the sparkline in the reverse data direction, choose Plot Data Right-to-Left from the menu. In Figure 10-2, the data range is in reverse date order (the most current date is to the left of the range). However, the context is historical, so we wanted to plot the sparklines with the value of the earliest date first and the most current date last. Therefore, we chose the option to plot the data from right to left.

✔ **Vertical axis minimum and maximum value options:** These options allow you to change the default behavior of the vertical axis.

You can't display a vertical axis on a sparkline (and one would be inappropriate on a sparkline), but you can make changes to an *implied* axis. The minimum and maximum value options are applicable to sparkline groups.

By default, Excel sets the vertical axis minimum and maximum values independently for each sparkline in a group. This option is appropriate if the sparkline data ranges have different orders of magnitude, or if comparisons among sparklines are unimportant. However, if the data ranges are of the same order of magnitude and comparison among sparklines is important, you can set the minimum and maximum values the same for all sparklines by selecting Same for All Sparklines from the menu.

Adding a New Data Series to a Chart

Follow these steps to add a new data series to a chart:

1. Activate the chart, click the Design contextual tab, and then click the Select Data button. Excel displays the Select Data Source dialog box (see Figure 10-3).

Figure 10-3

2. Click the Add button. Excel displays the Edit Series dialog box.

3. If the reference in the Series Name box is incorrect, clear the default entry and either type a name for the series or click the cell in the worksheet containing the series name. You can also leave the box blank.

4. If the reference in the Series Values box is incorrect, clear the default entry and select the series data range in the worksheet.

5. Click OK to return to the Select Data Source dialog box. The new series name (or a generic title if you didn't include a name in Step 3) appears in the Legend Entries window. In the window on the right side of the dialog box, Excel displays numbered category labels for the series. You can ignore these labels — Excel simply adds the new series to the chart using the existing category labels.

6. Click OK.

To quickly add a new data series to a chart, select the range that you want to add (including any label for the series name), and click the Copy button on the Ribbon's Home tab. Then activate the chart, click the arrow on the Paste button, and choose Paste Special from the menu. Excel opens the Paste Special dialog box. If necessary, modify the default settings and click OK.

Adding a Title to a Chart

The chart title normally appears at the top of the chart. When you create a chart, you can select a layout that includes a chart title box. To add a title to an existing chart, follow these steps:

1. Activate the chart and click the Layout tab to display the chart layout tools on the Ribbon.

2. Click the Chart Title button, and then choose an option from the menu. Excel adds a chart title box to the chart.

3. Click in the title box and type a title for the chart.

4. If you want to format the chart title, you can use the standard formatting options in the Font Group on the Ribbon's Home tab or you can use special WordArt and other formatting options on the Format tab.

Changing the Chart Type for an Existing Chart or Data Series

Excel supports a wide variety of chart types (line charts, column charts, and so on). After you create a chart, you might decide that a different chart type would better portray the data. You can even create a *combination* chart by selecting a different chart type for a data series. You can, for example, create a chart with one data series plotted as a line chart type and another data series plotted as a column chart type (see Figure 10-1).

To change the chart type for an existing chart or to change the chart type for a data series on a chart, follow these steps:

1. Activate the chart and click the Design tab to display the chart design tools on the Ribbon.

2. To change the chart type for the chart (this is, for all data series in the chart), click the Change Chart Type button. To change the chart type for a single data series, select the data series before clicking the Change Chart Type button. Excel displays the Change Chart Type dialog box.

3. In the list on the left, choose a chart type. Then in the gallery on the right, choose a chart subtype.

4. Click OK.

Creating a Chart

Excel provides several layout and formatting options that can save you time when you create a chart. Follow these steps to chart your data:

1. Select the data you want to chart, including any row and column labels (for category and series name identification).

2. Click the Insert tab on the Ribbon and then click a Chart Type button in the Charts group. Excel displays a chart subtype gallery.

3. Choose a subtype from the gallery. If you hover the mouse pointer over a chart type button or chart subtype gallery option, Excel displays a ScreenTip that provides assistance on how you can use the particular chart type or subtype.

After you choose a subtype, Excel creates a chart and displays the chart tools contextual tabs on the Ribbon and a header on the Excel title bar above the tabs. Excel automatically displays the tools for the Design tab on the Ribbon (see Figure 10-4).

Figure 10-4

4. If the layout of elements on the chart isn't what you want, choose a new layout from the Chart Layouts gallery. Use the upper arrows on the right side of the gallery to scroll the gallery display or the bottom arrow to display the entire gallery. Each layout includes a combination of typical elements for the chart. If you choose a layout that includes a chart title, click in the title box and type a title for the chart.

5. If required, select a new style for the chart from the Chart Styles gallery. Use the upper arrows on the right side of the gallery to scroll the gallery display or the bottom arrow to display the entire gallery. The styles in the gallery are based on the theme currently applied in the workbook, so if you change the theme, the styles change to match the new theme. *See also* "Formatting with Themes," in Part 1.

Figure 10-5 illustrates some important rules that Excel applies when creating a chart:

✔ If the data you're charting contains more rows than columns, Excel uses the row data to create the category axis. The row labels are used for category labels and the column labels are used for series names. (In Figure 10-5, see the data range A1:D13 and the resultant chart on the right of the range.)

If the row labels are missing or not included in the range, Excel labels the category axis with numbers. If, in addition, the column labels are missing or not included in the range, Excel names the series as Series 1, Series 2, and so on. (In Figure 10-5, see the data range A15:C26 and the resultant chart on the right of the range.)

✔ If the data you're charting contains more columns than rows, or an equal number of columns and rows, Excel uses the column data to create the category axis. The column labels are used for category labels and the row labels are used for series names. (In Figure 10-5, see the data range N1:Q3 and the resultant chart at the bottom of the range.)

✔ If the data you're charting contains only one series, Excel includes a chart title with the same name as the series name, assuming that a row or column label is available for the series name (as per the first rule).

Remember: You can reverse Excel's category and series name choices after the chart is created by activating the chart and clicking the Switch Row/Column button on the Design tab.

Figure 10-5

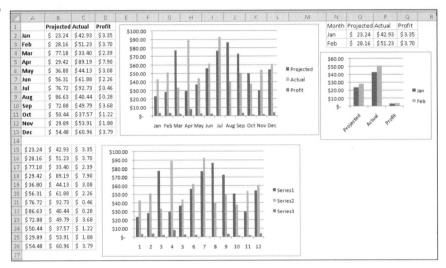

Creating and Using a Chart Template

A *chart template* is a standard chart (or combination chart) customized in a specific manner. You can subsequently use the template to create new charts. To customize a chart that you can save as a template, follow these steps:

1. Create a chart that's customized the way you want. For example, you can set colors or line styles, modify fonts and type sizes, and add a title.

2. Activate the chart and click the Design tab to display the chart design tools on the Ribbon.

3. Click the Save as Template button. Excel displays the Save Chart Template dialog box.

4. In the File Name box, enter a filename.

5. Click Save.

The template appears in the Templates category of the Change Chart Type dialog box (accessed by clicking the Change Chart Type button in the Design tab). After you select the Templates category, the new chart appears in the My Templates gallery on the right side of the dialog box. If you hover the mouse pointer over the chart, a ScreenTip displays the chart name you supplied in Step 4.

To use a template, *see* "Creating a Chart," earlier in this part, and choose the template from the Templates category.

Displaying a Data Table in a Chart

In Excel, you can display a table of the data that you use in the chart. The data table appears below the chart (see Figure 10-1). When you create a chart, you can select a layout that includes a data table.

To add a data table to an existing chart, follow these steps:

1. Activate the chart and click the Layout tab to display the chart layout tools on the Ribbon.

2. Click the Data Table button and choose an option from the menu. The data table appears below the chart.

3. To explore additional formatting options for the data table, choose More Data Table Options from the menu. Excel displays the Format Data Table dialog box.

4. Make your selections from the various formatting options and click OK.

Displaying Data Labels in a Chart

Sometimes you want your chart to display the data value for each point on the chart (see Figure 10-1). Or you want to display the category label for each data point. When you create a chart, you can select a layout that includes data labels.

To add data labels to a chart series, follow these steps:

1. Activate the chart and click the Layout tab to display the chart layout tools on the Ribbon.

2. Click one of the data points in the series. This action selects the entire data series.

   After you select the entire series, be careful not to click a data point because this action selects only a single data point. If you do accidentally select a single data point, click anywhere outside the data series and repeat this step.

3. Click the Data Labels button and choose an option from the menu. The data labels appear on the chart.

4. To explore additional formatting options for the data labels:

   a. Choose More Data Label Options from the menu. Excel displays the Format Data Labels dialog box.

   b. Make your selections from the various formatting options.

   c. Click OK.

Remember: The data labels are linked to the worksheet, so if your data changes, the labels change too. To override the data label with some other text, select the label and enter the new text (or even a cell reference) in the formula bar.

If Excel doesn't position the data labels correctly, select an individual label and drag it to a better location. To select an individual label, click the label twice.

Formatting a Chart Element

You can modify the elements in a chart in several ways. For example, you can change colors, line widths, and fonts. You make modifications in the Format dialog box, which varies for each type of chart element.

To modify an element in a chart, follow these steps:

1. Select the chart element. *See* "Selecting a Chart Element," later in this part.

2. Access the Format dialog box for the chart element that you selected by using any of the following techniques:

   - In the Current Selection group of the Layout tab, click the Format Selection button below the Chart Elements list.

   - Right-click the element and choose Format *Item Name* from the contextual menu that appears, where *Item Name* is the name of the chart element you select, such as Data Series, Gridlines, or Axis.

   - Double-click the element.

   - Press Ctrl+1 (the number 1).

3. Choose the option on the left side of the dialog box that corresponds to what you want to do.

4. Make the changes by selecting the appropriate options on the right side of the dialog box. For help on an option, click the help button (the question mark) in the dialog box.

5. Click OK.

Remember: You can change the color of some element parts — for example, the fill color or line color. You can select a theme color or a non-theme color. If you choose a theme color, the color changes if you change the workbook theme. If you choose a non-theme color, the color does not change if you change the workbook theme. *See also* "Formatting with Themes," in Part 1.

If you have several chart elements you want to format, leave the Format dialog box open. After you select a different element, the options in the Format dialog box change to those appropriate for the new element.

Handling Missing Data or Charting Hidden Data

Sometimes, data that you're charting may be missing one or more data points. Also, by default, Excel does not include data in hidden rows and columns within the data range you're charting. Excel offers several options for handling the missing data and allows you to chart hidden data in a range. Just follow these steps:

1. Activate the chart and click the Design tab to display the chart design tools on the Ribbon.

2. Click the Select Data button. Excel displays the Select Data Source dialog box.

3. Click the Hidden and Empty Cells button. Excel displays the Hidden and Empty Cell Settings dialog box.

4. Select the option that corresponds to how you want to handle the missing data:

   • **Gaps:** Excel ignores missing data, and the data series leaves a gap for each missing data point. This is the default setting.

   • **Zero:** Excel treats missing data as zero.

   • **Span with Line:** Excel calculates missing data by using data on either side of the missing point(s). This option is available only for line charts and some X Y scatter chart subtypes.

5. If you want to chart hidden data within the chart's source data range, select the Show Data in Hidden Rows and Columns check box.

6. Click OK to exit the Hidden and Empty Cell Settings dialog box, and click OK again to exit the Select Data Source dialog box.

Remember: The options that you set apply to the entire active chart; you can't set a different option for different series in the same chart.

Inserting and Modifying Chart Legends

A *legend* uses text and keys to describe the data series in a chart. A *key* is a small graphic that corresponds to the chart's series.

Adding a legend to a chart

When you create a chart, you can select a layout that includes a legend (labeled in Figure 10-1). If you don't include a legend as you create the chart, you can add one later. To add a legend to an existing chart, follow these steps:

1. Activate the chart and click the Layout tab to display the chart layout tools on the Ribbon.

2. Click the Legend button and choose an option from the menu. Excel displays the legend on the chart.

Changing the names (titles) on a chart legend

If you don't include row or column titles with the source data when you create a chart, Excel displays the default names (titles) *Series 1, Series 2,* and so on in the legend. To change the default names, follow these steps:

1. Activate the chart and click the Design tab to display the chart design tools on the Ribbon.

2. Click the Select Data button. You can also right-click the border area of the chart and choose Select Data from the contextual menu. Excel displays the Select Data Source dialog box.

3. Choose a name (*Series 1, Series 2,* and so on) in the Legend Entries (Series) window, and then click the Edit button above the series name. Excel displays the Edit Series dialog box.

4. Clear the entry in the Series Name box and either type a new name or point to a worksheet cell containing the name you want to use. Click OK to add the name and return to the Select Data Source dialog box.

5. Repeat Step 4 for each series that you want to rename.

6. Click OK to exit the Select Data Source dialog box.

Modifying a Chart Axis

After you create a chart, you may want to modify the value axis to change the scale, add an axis title, modify the tick mark display, add display units, and so on. Or you may want to modify the category axis to, for example, add a title, modify the tick marks, or change where the axis crosses the value axis.

Follow these steps to modify a chart axis:

1. Activate the chart and click the Layout tab to display the chart layout tools on the Ribbon.

2. Click the Axes button and choose a Horizontal Axis or Vertical Axis option, depending on which axis you want to modify. After you choose an axis option, a flyout menu appears.

3. If one of the standard options on the flyout menu is what you want, choose the option, and you're finished. Otherwise, continue with Step 4.

4. If none of the standard flyout menu options are what you want, choose More *<Axis>* Options at the bottom of the flyout menu, where *<Axis>* is the primary/secondary horizontal or primary/secondary vertical axis. Excel displays the Format Axis dialog box.

5. On the right side of the dialog box, select the axis options you want to change. For help, click the help button (the question mark at the top-right of the dialog box).

   You may have to experiment with the options to get what you want. You can always undo your selections (by clicking the undo button on the Quick Access toolbar) and start over if your chart doesn't show the expected results.

6. If you want to modify the axis formatting (number, fill, line, and so on), select one or more of the options in the list on the left side of the dialog box and select the appropriate options on the right.

7. Click OK when you are finished making your selections.

A quick way to modify an existing axis is by selecting and double-clicking the axis on the chart or by right-clicking the axis on the chart and choosing Format Axis from the menu. Proceed with Steps 5–7.

To add a title to an axis, activate the chart, click the Layout tab, and click the Axis Titles button. Choose an axis from the menu and choose a title option from the flyout menu. After Excel displays the axis title box on the chart, click in the box and enter a title.

Resizing, Moving, Copying, and Deleting an Embedded Chart

To resize an embedded chart, follow these steps:

1. Activate the chart.

2. Drag one of the eight resize handles (a series of dots) on the chart border to change the size of the element. When you hover the mouse pointer over a resize handle or when you drag the resize handle, the pointer changes into a black line with arrows on both ends.

You can move the embedded chart to a different location on the worksheet or you can make a copy of the chart on the worksheet:

✔ To move a chart using the mouse, first activate the chart. Then click the border of the chart between the resize handles, and drag the chart to the desired location in the worksheet. When you hover the mouse pointer over a border or when you drag the border, the pointer changes into a white arrow with a black cross on the arrow's tip.

✔ If you want to move a chart in small increments — for example, to line up multiple charts — it is difficult to do so using the mouse. In this case, you can use the arrow keys to move the chart. First make sure that the chart *isn't* activated. Press and hold the Ctrl key and then select the chart with the mouse. You can now move the chart using the arrow keys.

✔ To copy a chart, activate it. Then press and hold down the Ctrl key while dragging the chart. You can also use the Copy and Paste buttons on the Ribbon's Home tab or press Ctrl+C to copy and Ctrl+V to paste.

✔ To move the embedded chart to a separate chart sheet, select the chart, click the Design tab, and then click the Move Chart button. Specify the new location in the Move Chart dialog box and click OK. A chart sheet typically contains a single chart that is linked to the data in the worksheet.

To delete a chart, activate the chart and press the Delete key.

Resizing, Moving, and Deleting a Chart Element

You can resize the following chart elements: any titles and data labels, the legend, and the plot area. To resize a chart element, follow these steps:

1. Select the chart element that you want to resize.

2. Drag a resize handle (a square box or a circle) on the element border to change the size of the element. When you hover the mouse pointer over a resize handle, the pointer changes to a double-headed arrow. Clicking the mouse to drag the handle changes the pointer to a cross.

You can move the titles, the data labels, and the legend within the chart area. To move a chart element, follow these steps:

1. Select the chart element that you want to move.

2. Click the border of the element between the resize handles, and drag the element to the desired location in the chart. When you hover the mouse pointer over a border or when you drag the border, the pointer changes to a cross with an arrow on each end.

You can delete any element in a chart, including a data series. To delete a chart element, follow these steps:

1. Select the element that you want to delete.

2. Press the Delete key.

See also "Selecting a Chart Element," immediately following this section.

Selecting a Chart Element

Modifying an element in a chart is similar to everything else that you do in Excel: First you make a selection — in this case, select a chart element — and then you issue a command to do something with the selection.

You can select a chart element in any of the following three ways:

- ✔ Click the chart element. If the element is a series, clicking the series once selects all the points in the series. Clicking the series twice selects individual points in the series.

- ✔ Press the up-arrow or down-arrow key to cycle through all the elements in the chart. If a data series is selected, you can press the right-arrow or left-arrow key to select individual points in the series.

- ✔ Select the chart and click the Layout tab on the Ribbon. Select a chart element from the Chart Elements drop-down list (located above the Format Selection button) in the Current Selection group. This option is useful if you find it difficult to select the element with the mouse.

 TIP If you move the mouse pointer over a chart element, a ScreenTip displays the name of the element. If the element is a data point, the ScreenTip displays the value. The ScreenTip is useful in ensuring that you're selecting the intended element.

Updating the Source Data Range for a Chart or a Data Series

Often, you create a chart that uses a particular range of data and then extend the data range by adding new data in the worksheet. If you add new data to a range, the data series in the chart doesn't update to include the new data. Or you may delete some of the data in a range that you used to create the chart. If you delete data from a range, by default the chart displays the deleted data as zero values.

To update the entire chart to reflect the new data range, follow these steps:

1. Activate the chart, and then click the Design tab to display the chart design tools on the Ribbon.

2. Click the Select Data button to display the Select Data Source dialog box.

3. In the Chart Data Range box, manually edit the source data reference or clear the box and use the mouse pointer to select the new range on the worksheet.

4. Click OK, and Excel updates the chart with the new data range.

If you need to update the range for a single data series on the chart, follow these steps:

1. Activate the chart, and then click the Design tab to display the chart design tools on the Ribbon.

2. Click the Select Data button. Excel displays the Select Data Source dialog box.

3. Select the series name of the series you want to modify in the Legend Entries (Series) window, and click the Edit button above the window. Excel displays the Edit Series dialog box.

4. In the Series Values box, manually edit the source data reference, or clear the box and use the mouse pointer to select the new range in the worksheet. Click OK to return to the Select Data Source dialog box.

5. If necessary, modify the range for category labels. Click the Edit button under Horizontal (Categories) Axis Labels to display the Axis Labels dialog box. In the Axis Label Range box, manually edit the category labels reference, or clear the box and select the new range on the worksheet.

6. Click OK, and Excel updates the chart with the new data range.

 After you activate a chart, Excel outlines in the worksheet the ranges that the chart uses. To extend or reduce the range of the entire chart, simply drag an outline handle (a small square box on the corner of the outline). To extend or reduce the range of a data series, select the data series in the chart and drag an outline handle.

 A better way to handle data ranges that change is to convert the range to a *table*. After you add or remove data from a table, the chart created from the range (either before or after you convert the range to a table) updates automatically. **See also** Part 11, "Working with Tables."

Working with Tables

A *table* is a structure that you can use as a data source for reports and charts that you create in Excel. You can also analyze data in the table directly, because it provides powerful filtering, sorting, and formatting tools. Data for the table can be entered manually, copied from another worksheet, or imported from external sources such as a text file, the Web, an XML file, or a database.

In this part . . .

- ✔ **Creating a Table**
- ✔ **Formatting a Table**
- ✔ **Inserting and Deleting Table Rows and Columns**
- ✔ **Referencing Table Data in a Formula**
- ✔ **Removing Duplicate Values from a Table**

Anatomy of a Table

A table consists of rows and columns of data. Each column of data has a name, such as First Name, Last Name, City, or State. The names appear in the table's *header* row. You can use a table as a data source for reports and charts. Charts are updated automatically if you add or remove data from the table or filter data in the table. Excel also provides many handy tools that allow you to analyze data in the table. For example, you can easily sort and filter data, format the table conditionally to highlight specific data (for example, poor, fair, good), and add formula columns to aid in analysis. You can create data for a table manually, copy data from a worksheet, link data from a worksheet or a different workbook, or import data from an external source. If you have data in your worksheet that is arranged in a list like that shown in Figure 11-1, consider converting the list to a table to take advantage of a table's many convenient features.

Header row   Column header   Table tools tab header   Table header in column header

Figure 11-1

Total row   Data rows

The following is a description of the parts of a table:

- ✔ **Table area:** The header row, data rows, and optional totals row.

- ✔ **Header row:** Names shared by all data rows — for example, Customer Name, Order ID, and Unit Price.

- ✔ **Drop-down sort and filter arrow:** Found in each column in the header row. Clicking the arrow displays sort and filter options for the column.

- ✔ **Data row:** Specific information derived from the columns in the header row, such as transaction information (for example, details of sales), customer data, or product data.

- ✔ **Totals row:** Allows you to perform a calculation (such as Sum, Average, or Count) on any column of data.

Tables often contain more rows that can be displayed simultaneously on the screen. If the cell pointer is in the table and you scroll the worksheet so that the header row is no longer displayed in the worksheet window, the header titles appear in the column header area (see Figure 11-1).

The display of the column drop-down arrows in the column header area is new in Excel 2010.

See also "Familiarizing Yourself with the Excel 2010 Window," in Part 1.

Converting a Table to a Range

If you no longer need to work with a table, you can convert the table to a normal range. Right-click in the table and choose Table⇨Convert to Range from the contextual menu or click anywhere in the table and then click Convert to Range on the Table Tools Design tab.

Creating a Table

You can create a table from a data range that is set up with a header row. If your range does not include a header row, you should add one. ***See also*** Part 4, "Entering and Editing Worksheet Data." Follow these steps to create a table from a range:

1. Select any cell in the range.

2. Click the Insert tab on the Ribbon and then click the Table button (or press Ctrl+L). Excel displays the Create Table dialog box and selects the entire contiguous range that includes the active cell pointer.

3. Click OK. Excel creates the table, applies a default style, and adds a sort and filter arrow to the cells in the header row. Excel also displays the Table Tools Design tab on the Ribbon.

Formatting a Table

When you create a table, Excel applies a default style to the table. However, you can apply a different predefined style to the table or create a style from scratch. You can also apply formatting based on the contents of a cell or table column.

Applying a new style to a table

Excel identifies the following specific areas in a table that you can format automatically and independently: the header row, data rows, totals row, first column, and last column. Follow these steps to apply a new style to a table:

1. Click any cell in the table and then click the Design tab.

2. Select a new style from the Table Styles gallery. You can scroll the gallery options by clicking the upper (scroll) arrows on the right side of the gallery, or you can display a drop-down grid by clicking the arrow below the scroll arrows. You can preview a style by hovering the mouse pointer over a style. Click a style option to apply a style.

3. In addition, or as an alternative, to Step 2, you can select style and display options from the Table Style Options group. Click to select or deselect the appropriate check boxes.

Remember: The styles you apply from the Table Styles gallery are based on the theme applied to the workbook. Therefore, if you change the workbook theme, both the table style and gallery styles change to match the new theme. *See also* "Formatting with Themes," in Part 1.

Formatting based on cell or column content

Formatting a table based on the contents of a cell or column contents (conditional formatting) is similar to formatting a non-table cell or range based on the contents of the cell or range. *See* "Formatting Based on the Contents of a Cell or Range," and "Formatting a Range Using Comparative Visualizations," both in Part 8.

However, note the following when you apply conditional formatting to a table:

> ✔ If you apply conditional formatting to an entire column, the formatting for the column is automatically extended if you add new rows to the table.

> ✔ Formatting is applied to a table in the following order: direct formatting (for example, formatting you apply from the Font group on the Ribbon's Home tab) appears over table style formatting, and conditional formatting appears over direct formatting. For example, if you remove direct formatting, any table formatting is still there. Similarly, if you remove conditional formatting, any direct formatting is still applied.

Inserting a Totals Row in a Table

When you create a table, by default Excel does not include the totals row. However, if you need to total data in your table columns, you can add a totals row easily. Make sure that the cell pointer is in the table range, click the Design tab, and select the Totals Row check box in the Table Style Options group.

After you click the mouse pointer in a cell of the totals row, Excel adds a drop-down arrow to the cell. Clicking the arrow displays a convenient list of common functions you can apply (Sum, Average, Count, Standard Deviation, and so on). If you want to use a function that is not listed, you can choose the More Functions option and select the function in the Insert Function dialog box.

Inserting and Deleting Table Rows and Columns

You may need to insert new rows into a table to add data. Also, you may want to add a column to perform a calculation based on other columns in the table. Excel provides convenient methods for inserting rows and columns. You can also delete table rows and columns you no longer need.

Adding and deleting table rows

Choose one of the following methods to add rows to a table:

> ✔ To add a row above an existing table row (including the totals row), right-click a cell in the existing table row and choose Insert⇨ Table Rows Above. If you right-click a cell in the last data row, you can add a row above or below the last row.

> ✔ If you use the Tab key to move to the next column when entering data in a row, Excel adds a new row automatically after you press the Tab key in the *rightmost* column of the *last* data row.

✔ If a blank row is immediately below the last data row, you can enter data in any cell in the blank row and Excel will add the row to the table. Table formatting (normal and conditional) and any column formulas are extended to include the new row.

To delete a table row, right-click any cell in the row and choose Delete⇨Table Rows from the contextual menu. To delete multiple rows, select the rows, right-click within the selection and choose Delete⇨Table Rows.

Adding and deleting table columns

Choose one of the following methods to add columns to a table:

✔ To add a column to the left of an existing table column, right-click a cell in the existing table column, and then choose Insert⇨Table Columns to the Left from the contextual menu. If you right-click a cell in the rightmost table column, you can add a column to the left or right of the rightmost column. Excel provides a generic title for the column header that you can change to a more meaningful name.

✔ If a blank column is immediately to the right of the rightmost column, you can enter data in any cell in the blank column and Excel will add the column to the table. The table formatting is extended to the new column.

To delete a table column, right-click any cell in the column and choose Delete⇨Table Columns from the contextual menu. To delete multiple columns, select the columns, right-click within the selection, and choose Delete⇨Table Columns.

Remember: You cannot add individual cells to or remove individual cells from a table. You can add or remove only entire table rows or entire table columns.

Referencing Table Data in a Formula

In Excel, a table has a well-defined structure with identifiable parts, such as the entire table, the header row, the data area, and named columns. (*See* "Anatomy of a Table," earlier in this part.) As such, you can reference various parts of a table by name instead of by the usual row and column references. When you create a table, Excel provides a generic name for the table (Table1, Table2 and so on). If you intend to reference table data in a formula using named table elements, you should change the name to something more descriptive, such as SalesData. To change Excel's default table name, select any cell in the table, click the Design tab on the Ribbon, and enter a new name in the Table Name text box (located in the Properties group). The following rules apply to table and column names:

    ✔ The table name must be different from any other names you create in the workbook and must follow Excel's name creation rules. **_See also_** Part 6, "Creating and Using Names."

    ✔ Column names must be unique within the table, although different tables can have the same column names.

    ✔ If a table name or column name changes, formulas that reference the name automatically update to include the new name.

    ✔ Excel updates table and column name references automatically as rows and columns are added to or removed from the table.

The reference that includes the table name and any of its identifiable parts is called a *structured reference*. The identifiable parts are also known as *specifiers*.

A structured reference can be unqualified or fully qualified. An *unqualified reference* does not include the table name. A *fully qualified reference* must include the table name.

Referencing table data outside the table

You must use a *fully qualified* structured reference when you reference table data in a formula that's outside the table range. Use the following methods to reference table data in a formula:

    ✔ To reference all the data in the table, use the table name, or the table name and the #Data specifier. If you want to sum all the data in a table named SalesData, for example, enter

      `=SUM(SalesData) or SUM(SalesData[#Data])`

      In the formula, `SalesData[#Data]` represents the structured reference.

      Note that the SUM function ignores any text in the structured reference.

    ✔ To reference the data in a table column, use the table name and a column qualifier in the form `TableName[ColumnName]`. For example, if you want to sum a column named Quarter1 in a table named SalesData, enter

      `=SUM(SalesData[Quarter1])`

    ✔ Other table references are useful for some types of lookup formulas. To reference an entire table (the header row and all data rows), use the form `TableName[#All]`. To reference table headers only, use the form `TableName[#Headers]`. To reference an entire column (header and data) use the form `TableName[[#All], [ColumnName]]`. To reference just the header text of a column, use `TableName [[#Headers], [ColumnName]]`.

      If you include a totals row in your table, you can reference a total by using the form `TableName[[#Totals], [ColumnName]]`.

TIP

You can save time entering table name references in a formula by using the Formula AutoComplete feature, which lists the defined table names as you begin entering the name in the formula. After you enter a square bracket ([) following the table name, the AutoComplete feature lists the available specifiers (#All, #Totals, #Data, and so on). *See also* "Entering formulas manually," in Part 4.

Referencing table data using a calculated column

A *calculated column* (sometimes called a *calculated field*) is simply a column that you add to the table that references table data in a formula. The formula references are similar to those in "Referencing table data outside the table," in the preceding section, except you can use an *unqualified* structured reference because the calculated column is part of the table.

Follow these steps to add a calculated column and add a formula:

1. Add a new column to the table. *See* "Inserting and Deleting Table Rows and Columns," earlier in this part.

2. Enter a formula that references the table in any cell of the new column. You can enter the formula manually or by pointing with the mouse. For example, if you have a table named *SalesData* and want to calculate the difference between the sales figures in the *Quarter1* and *Quarter2* columns, enter the following manually:

```
=[Quarter1]-[Quarter2]
```

Note that after you enter the formula in the column, Excel evaluates the formula; that is, Excel uses an *implicit intersection* for each row.

If you instead enter the formula by pointing, Excel qualifies the column reference with an at sign (@) and brackets the combined reference. For example:

```
=[@[Quarter1]]-[[@Quarter2]]
```

To enter the formula by pointing with the mouse, type the equal sign (=), point to the Quarter1 column in the *same* row as the formula you're entering, type the minus sign (–) and point to the Quarter2 column. As you type and point with the mouse, Excel completes the formula. See Figure 11-2.

EXCEL 2010

2010

The @ character is shorthand for the [#ThisRow], specifier and is new in Excel 2010.

Excel uses the [#ThisRow], (@) specifier to evaluate the formula using *explicit intersection*. Either form of the formula (implicit or explicit intersection) returns the same result.

3. After you complete the formula, press Enter. Excel fills the entire column with the formula.

Figure 11-2

	A	B	C	D	E	F	G	H	I
1	Region	Quarter 1	Quarter 2	Quarter 3	Quarter 4	Q1-Q2			
2	North East	$ 166,761	$ 131,967	$ 129,478	$ 91,724	=[@[Quarter 1]]-[@[Quarter 2]]			
3	North West	$ 97,596	$ 103,241	$ 184,599	$ 141,495				
4	North	$ 109,825	$ 155,302	$ 136,108	$ 102,426				
5	South East	$ 166,605	$ 147,629	$ 128,881	$ 147,856				
6	South West	$ 153,003	$ 182,066	$ 155,004	$ 111,317				
7	South	$ 85,012	$ 190,246	$ 81,851	$ 134,675				
8	Est	$ 197,160	$ 104,534	$ 116,112	$ 89,883				
9	West	$ 121,007	$ 180,793	$ 94,066	$ 199,835				
10	Central	$ 189,920	$ 192,535	$ 96,921	$ 113,896				

Remember: If you change the formula in any cell of a calculated column, Excel updates the formulas in all other cells in the column automatically. If you do not want Excel to update all other cells in the column, click the Smart Tag (the lightning bolt icon with the drop-down arrow) that appears next to the column after you update the formula and choose Undo Calculated Column from the menu.

Removing Duplicate Values from a Table

If you have a table with duplicated information, you might want to remove the rows containing the duplicates before analyzing the data. Excel provides many convenient options for removing duplicated data. For example, you can choose to remove duplicates if the entire row is duplicated (the default option) or you can choose to remove rows if the data in one or more columns is duplicated. Follow these steps to remove duplicated data from your table:

1. Click any cell in the table, and then click the Design tab on the Ribbon.

2. Click the Remove Duplicates button. Excel selects the entire data area of the table and displays the Remove Duplicates dialog box (see Figure 11-3).

Figure 11-3

3. If you want to remove rows in which all column data is duplicated, click OK. If you want to remove rows in which only data in one or more columns is duplicated (for example, a last name), select the column or columns and click OK.

The duplicated data is removed from the table permanently. If the result of the removal operation is not what you want, you can undo the operation (click the undo button on the Quick Access toolbar or press Ctrl+Z) and start over.

If you want to retain your original data, you can select and copy the table to another worksheet. If you have a particularly large data range, make a copy of the worksheet instead of copying the table data.

Remember: You can remove duplicates in an ordinary (non-table) range. Select the range and click the Remove Duplicates button on the Ribbon's Data tab.

Remember: If a column has date or numeric data, Excel uses the number formatting in the column to determine whether data is duplicated. For example, Excel does not consider the dates 12/31/2010 and Friday, December 31, 2010 to be duplicates, although internally it stores both representations identically.

Selecting Table Areas

Excel provides convenient methods for you to select table rows, table columns, or the entire table. These methods are particularly useful if, for example, you want to copy table data or move the table to another location or format entire columns conditionally:

 ✔ To select a table row, move the mouse pointer to the leftmost column in the row until the pointer changes into a right-pointing arrow. Then click the mouse to select the row. You can select a table row also by selecting any cell in the row and pressing Shift+spacebar.

 ✔ To select the data cells in a table column, move the mouse pointer to the header row until the pointer changes into a down-pointing arrow. Then click the mouse to select the data cells. If you want to select the entire table column, including the header and totals cells, click the mouse again. You can select the data cells of a table column also by selecting any cell in the column and pressing Ctrl+spacebar. Pressing Ctrl+spacebar again selects the entire table column.

 ✔ To select all data rows in a table, move the mouse pointer to the upper-left cell in the header row until the mouse changes into a diagonal arrow, and then click to select the data rows. Click the mouse again to select the entire table. You can select all data rows in the table also by pressing Ctrl+Shift+spacebar. Press Ctrl+Shift+spacebar again to select the entire table. Another way to select the entire table is to select any cell in the table and move the mouse pointer to any edge of the table until the pointer changes to an arrow with a cross at the tip. Then click to select the table.

Analyzing Data with PivotTables

A *PivotTable* report (or simply a *PivotTable*) is an interactive table that organizes and summarizes raw data. The PivotTable allows you summarize, filter, and view data in multiple dimensions to assist in your analysis.

In this part . . .

- ✔ Adding a Slicer Report Filter
- ✔ Creating PivotTables and PivotCharts
- ✔ Creating and Formatting a PivotTable Report

Anatomy of a PivotTable

In contrast to a table, in which you present and analyze the details of your data, a PivotTable enables you to present and analyze your data in a summarized form. Moreover, with a PivotTable (see Figure 12-1), you can view different dimensions of your summarized data in hierarchical levels of detail.

Slicer Header   Row labels   PivotTable Tools tab header   PivotTable field list track pane

Slicer   Report filter   Column label   Row grand totals   PivotTable field list

Figure 12-1

Field items filter buttons   Field items   Slicer   Clear filter button   Subtotal   Values area   Column grand totals   PivotTable label boxes

The following is a description of the elements in a PivotTable:

✔ **PivotTable Field List task pane:** Displayed after you indicate that you want to create a PivotTable from the source data. The task pane includes the field labels (column titles) from the source data and boxes that correspond to areas on the PivotTable.

- ✔ **Row labels:** Fields that you want to summarize in rows.

- ✔ **Field Item:** An individual item in the row or column areas of the PivotTable.

- ✔ **Column labels:** Fields that you want to summarize in columns.

- ✔ **Values:** The data being summarized (for example, Sum of TotalPrice).

- ✔ **Report filter:** One or more of the fields in the Field List task pane used to filter the PivotTable report.

- ✔ **Slicer:** An interactive filter, similar to the report filter but having additional functionality.

Remember: To construct a PivotTable report, at a minimum you need to choose a field to summarize in the data area and one field for either the row or column area. Your choices depend on how you want to view your data.

Remember: The source data that feeds the PivotTable is held in an area of system memory known as a *PivotCache.* If you have sufficient memory and the source data comes from an external data source, you may able to create a PivotTable from source data that has more rows or columns than Excel supports. This is possible if, after summarization, the data fits within Excel's row and column limits.

Adding a Slicer Report Filter

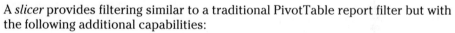

A *slicer* provides filtering similar to a traditional PivotTable report filter but with the following additional capabilities:

- ✔ You can attach a slicer to more than one PivotTable, allowing you to filter multiple PivotTables simultaneously.

- ✔ A slicer displays the list of items that are filtered and unfiltered. A report filter can display only one filtered item at a time.

- ✔ You can drag a slicer anywhere on the worksheet or copy the slicer to another worksheet in the workbook. A report filter occupies a fixed area in the PivotTable and cannot be moved.

Unless you need to maintain backward compatibility with earlier versions of Excel, a slicer is usually preferable to a report filter.

Creating a new slicer

You can create one or more slicers at the same time. Each slicer represents a field in the PivotTable field list and displays the items in the field. You can create a slicer for a field whether or not the field is already used in the PivotTable.

Follow these steps to create one or more slicers:

1. Click anywhere in the PivotTable and then click the PivotTable Tools Option tab.

2. In the Sort & Filter group, click the top part of the Insert Slicer button. Excel displays the Insert Slicers dialog box (see Figure 12-2).

Figure 12-2

3. Select the check boxes for the field or fields you want to use to filter the PivotTable. Excel displays the slicer or slicers on the worksheet (refer to Figure 12-1, where we've created State/Province and Region slicers).

Copying, moving, deleting, and resizing a slicer

After you create a slicer, you can organize its location and size as follows:

✔ To move a slicer, simply hover the mouse pointer over the slicer until a black cross-arrow appears at the tip of the pointer. Then hold down the left mouse button and drag to the new location.

✔ To copy a slicer to another worksheet, right-click anywhere in the slicer and choose Copy from the menu (or select the slicer by clicking the header area and pressing Ctrl+C). Select the new worksheet, right-click anywhere, and choose Paste from the Paste Options gallery in the menu (or press Ctrl+V).

✔ To delete a slicer, select the slicer by clicking the header area and pressing Delete.

✔ To resize a slicer, hover the mouse pointer over an edge or the middle of a side until the pointer changes to a double-sided arrow. Then hold down the left mouse button and drag to resize.

Filtering a PivotTable with a slicer

As shown in Figure 12-1, a slicer displays a list of all the items in a field. If there are more items than the slicer can display simultaneously, you can use the scroll bar to the right of the slicer or resize the slicer to see additional items. You can use a slicer to filter a PivotTable in the following ways:

✔ To filter a single item, just click the item in the slicer.

✔ To filter nonconsecutive items, click the first item in the slicer, press and hold Ctrl, and select the other items.

✔ To filter consecutive items, click the first item in the slicer, press and hold Shift, and click the last item. Alternatively, click the first item and drag with the mouse to the last item.

✔ To clear all filters that are set in a slicer, click the Clear Filter button on the right side of the slicer header (refer to Figure 12-1).

Excel excludes all unfiltered items from the PivotTable. Note also that filtered and unfiltered items have different background colors.

Formatting a slicer

If you want to include a slicer in a report, you might want to change the default formatting. A typical report might include one or more PivotCharts and associated slicers. Because a PivotChart is associated with a PivotTable, filtering the PivotTable also filters the PivotChart. *See also* "Creating and Using a PivotChart," later in this part.

Follow these steps to format a slicer:

1. Click the slicer header to select it. Excel displays the Slicer Tools contextual tab on the Ribbon.

2. Click the Options tab if it isn't already selected. In the Slicer Styles group, select a style from the gallery. Click the arrow at the bottom right of the gallery to display all available styles.

3. Click a new style from the gallery. The slicer formatting changes to reflect the new style.

4. If you don't like any of the available styles, choose New Slicer Style at the bottom of the available styles gallery. Excel displays the New Slicer Quick Style dialog box (see Figure 12-3).

Figure 12-3

5. Provide a name for the style in the Name box.

6. Select an element to format in the Slicer Element list box. Then click Format to display the Format Slicer Element dialog box.

7. Select formatting options from the available tabs. Your choices are Font, Border, and Fill.

8. Click OK to return to the New Slicer Quick Style dialog box. Repeat Steps 6 and 7 for other slicer elements you want to format.

9. After you complete your formatting changes, click OK to exit the New Slicer Quick Style dialog box. The new style appears in the Custom section of the Styles gallery.

In many cases, you may want to change the format of elements in an existing style instead of creating a new style from scratch. In Step 4 of the preceding procedure, instead of choosing New Slicer Style, right-click the style you want to modify and choose Duplicate from the menu. Excel displays the Modify Quick Style dialog box. Continue from Step 5 to select the elements you want to modify.

Remember: You can't directly change a built-in style, but you can create a duplicate of a built-in style and make the changes in the duplicate.

Associating a slicer with other PivotTables

After you create a new slicer for a PivotTable, you can associate the slicer with other PivotTables in the workbook. The other PivotTables *must* share the same data source as the original PivotTable. The simplest way to associate a slicer with another PivotTable is to create one or more copies of the original PivotTable. If you already created multiple copies of a PivotTable before you add a slicer, by default the slicer is associated with only the PivotTable you used to create the slicer.

Follow these steps to associate a slicer with another copy of a PivotTable:

1. Create one or more copies of the PivotTable if you did not already do so. *See* "Copying a PivotTable," later in this part.

2. Select the slicer you want to associate with the PivotTable copy or copies.

3. Click the Slicer Tools Options tab and then click the PivotTable Connections button. Alternatively, you can right-click the slicer and choose PivotTable Connections from the contextual menu. Excel displays the PivotTable Connections dialog box.

4. In the dialog box, place a check mark in the box next to the name of each PivotTable you want to associate with the slicer. The dialog box also displays the worksheet that contains each PivotTable in the list.

5. Click OK after you complete your selections.

Changing the Summarization of PivotTable Data

When you add a numeric field to the values area of a PivotTable, by default Excel uses the Sum function to summarize the data. If you add a text field to the values area, Excel uses the Count function to summarize the text data. The Count function is the only way to summarize text data, but Excel provides several alternative options for summarizing numeric data. Use either of the following methods to select a different summarization function for a numeric field:

✔ Right-click within the numeric field in the values area of the PivotTable, choose Summarize Data By from the contextual menu, and then choose an option from the flyout menu. Excel displays the new summary for the selected field.

✔ Select any cell within the numeric field in the values area of the PivotTable, click the PivotTable Options tab on the Ribbon, click the Summarize Data By button, and then choose an option from the menu.

You can display different summarizations for the same numeric field in the PivotTable (for example, Sum and Average). For each new summarization, simply drag the field label from the field list in the task pane to the Values box (the Values box can have the same field multiple times). Each time you drag the field to the Values box, Excel adds the field to the values area of the PivotTable using the default summarization. To change the default, use the procedure outlined for changing the summarization.

Copying a PivotTable

Sometimes you want to use different views with a PivotTable — say for analyzing the PivotTable data directly, for referencing specific PivotTable data in a formula, or for displaying different PivotCharts. It would be tedious if you had to constantly drag fields on and off the PivotTable every time you needed a different view of the data. Instead, you can create one or more copies of the PivotTable and arrange the fields the way you want on each copy. Use either of the following methods to copy a PivotTable:

✔ The quickest way to create a copy of a PivotTable is to copy the worksheet in which the PivotTable is located. You can make as many copies of the worksheet as you need. **See** "Copying a Worksheet," in Part 3.

✔ If you have multiple PivotTables in a worksheet but need to copy only one of the PivotTables, follow these steps:

1. Click anywhere in the PivotTable and click the PivotTable Tools Options tab.

2. In the Actions group, click the arrow at the end of the Select button and choose Entire PivotTable from the menu. Excel highlights the entire PivotTable.

3. Right-click in the PivotTable and choose Copy from the contextual menu, or press Ctrl+C.

4. Select the destination worksheet and the location for the upper-left cell of the PivotTable row area.

5. Right-click and choose Paste from the Paste Options gallery in the contextual menu.

Creating and Using a PivotChart

It's difficult to detect trends and patterns when you're working with PivotTable data, even when the data is highly summarized. To help with this endeavor, you can create a PivotChart. You can choose to create a PivotChart at the same time you create a PivotTable.

PivotCharts are similar to standard Excel charts but with the following differences:

✔ The PivotChart is interactive. You can filter and adjust fields directly in the PivotChart. Any change you make to the PivotChart is reflected in the underlying PivotTables.

✔ Any subtotals and totals in the PivotTable are not included in the chart.

✔ The chart series are based on columnar data in the values area of the chart. The series cannot be in rows. Furthermore, the column labels are used for the series names. (Refer to Figure 12-1.)

✔ The field items in the row area of the PivotTable are used for category labels. (Refer to Figure 12-1.)

✔ PivotCharts do not support X Y scatter, bubble and stock chart types.

If you are unfamiliar with some of the terminology used in this section, see "Anatomy of a Chart," in Part 10.

Creating a PivotChart

Follow the steps for "Creating a PivotTable Report," immediately following in this part. However, in Step 2, select the arrow part of the PivotTable button and then choose PivotChart from the menu. A PivotChart cannot exist without an associated PivotTable, so Excel creates a PivotTable with the PivotChart. Because you don't specify a chart type when you create a PivotChart in this manner, Excel uses its default chart type (2-D column chart) and default chart formatting. If you want to change the chart type, follow the steps for "Changing the Chart Type for an Existing Chart or Data Series," in Part 10.

Note that the PivotChart is blank until you add fields to the PivotTable.

Alternatively, you can create a PivotChart after you create the PivotTable by following these steps:

1. Click anywhere within the PivotTable and then click the PivotChart button on the PivotTable Tools Options tab.

2. In the Insert Chart dialog box, choose the chart category on the left and the chart style on the right. Click OK to create the chart.

Using a PivotChart

After you create a PivotChart, you can use it interactively. The chart includes embedded field buttons, and the position of the field buttons corresponds roughly to the field locations in the PivotTable. See Figure 12-4.

In Figure 12-4, we used the Product Category button on the chart to filter out the Accessories and Clothing categories.

You can remove some or all filter buttons on the chart. To remove all buttons, select the chart, click the PivotChart Tools Analyze tab on the Ribbon, and then click the icon portion of the Field Buttons split button. To remove buttons that correspond to the Row, Column, Values, or Report Filter area of the PivotTable, click the label and arrow portion of the Field Buttons split button and then clear the appropriate check boxes on the menu.

Figure 12-4

Note that on the chart, the area corresponding to the PivotTable Row area is called the Axis area (the horizontal axis) and the area corresponding to the PivotTable Column area is called the Legend area.

Creating a PivotTable Report

The data for your PivotTable can come from an external data source (such as a database) or an Excel range or table. *See also* Part 11, "Working with Tables." Although you can create a PivotTable from an ordinary (non-table) worksheet range, using a table is preferable — if the table expands or shrinks, after you refresh the PivotTable, the data for it is based on the new table range.

To create a PivotTable report from a table, follow these steps:

1. Move the cell pointer to any cell in the table.

2. Click the Insert tab on the Ribbon and then click the top part of the PivotTable button. Excel displays the Create Pivot Table dialog box and outlines the table's data area. Excel inserts the table name in the Table/Range box.

3. In the lower half of the dialog box, specify where you want to locate the PivotTable and then click OK. If you select the Existing Worksheet option, click the Location box and then click the cell in the worksheet that will be the upper-left corner of the PivotTable. Excel displays the PivotTable Field List task pane and the area on the worksheet that will hold the PivotTable. In addition, Excel displays PivotTable tools contextual tabs on the Ribbon.

4. In the Field List task pane, select the check boxes next to the field labels of the fields that you want to include or drag the field labels to the boxes in the lower portion of the task pane. These boxes correspond to the label areas in the PivotTable where your selected fields will appear (refer to Figure 12-1).

If you select check boxes, Excel chooses the boxes in the lower portion of the task pane to place the field labels based on the following assumptions:

- Field labels for numeric fields (such as TotalPrice) are placed in the Values box.

- Field labels for non-numeric fields are placed in the Row Labels box.

To override Excel's default behavior, drag the field labels from the list in the top window to the appropriate boxes in the lower part of the task pane.

After Excel places field labels in the boxes (or you drag the labels to the boxes manually), the field data appears in the appropriate PivotTable label areas on the worksheet. By default, field labels in the Values box sum the corresponding data that appears in the values area of the PivotTable.

Figure 12-1 demonstrates the hierarchical nature of summarizing data in a PivotTable and the relationship between the arrangement of the fields in the task pane and the worksheet display.

Excel provides + and − indicators next to each level header on the worksheet, so you can quickly expand or collapse a level of detail in the PivotTable summary. Furthermore, when you create a PivotTable, Excel displays the PivotTable in a Compact view by default. The Compact view is similar to that shown in Figure 12-1, except field headers (labels) are not displayed. To see the field labels, click the drop-down arrow to the right of Row Labels or Column Labels.

See also "Modifying a PivotTable's Structure," later in this part.

Formatting a PivotTable Report

When you create a PivotTable, Excel applies a default style to the PivotTable. However, you can apply a different predefined style to the PivotTable or create a new style. You can also apply formatting based on the contents of a cell or a PivotTable field.

Applying a new style to a PivotTable

Follow these steps to apply a new predefined style to a PivotTable:

1. Click any cell in the PivotTable and then click the Design tab.

2. Select a new style from the PivotTable Styles gallery. Scroll the gallery options by clicking the upper (scroll) arrows on the right side of the gallery, or display a drop-down grid by clicking the arrow below the scroll arrows. Preview a style by hovering the mouse pointer over the style.

3. In addition, or as an alternative, to Step 2, you can select style and display options from the PivotTable Style Options group. Select or deselect the appropriate check boxes.

Remember: The styles you apply from the PivotTable Styles gallery are based on the theme applied to the workbook. Therefore, if you change the workbook theme, the applied PivotTable style and the gallery styles change to match the new theme. *See also* "Formatting with Themes," in Part 1.

Formatting based on data values

Formatting a PivotTable based on data values (conditional formatting) is similar to formatting a non-PivotTable cell or range based on the contents of the cell or range. *See* "Formatting Based on the Contents of a Cell or Range" and "Formatting a Range using Comparative Visualizations," both in Part 8.

After you select a cell or range of cells in the values area and apply a conditional formatting rule, a Formatting Options Smart Tag (a small icon to the right of the selection) appears (see Figure 12-5).

Figure 12-5

Years			
2009	2010	Grand Total	
$7,560.00	9,360.00	$16,920.00	
$6,996.00	*Apply formatting rule to ...*		
$8,225.35			
$1,232.25	○ Selected cells		
$8,857.94	○ All cells showing "Sum of SalesAmount" values		
$31,595.97	○ All cells showing "Sum of SalesAmount" values for "Product Subcategory" and "Years"		
$5,993.91	$9,018.36	$15,012.27	
$37,789.74	$50,979.99	$88,769.73	
$108,251.16	$148,170.91	$256,422.07	

Clicking the Smart Tag provides the following options:

- ✔ Selected cells: This is the default option. Excel applies the conditional formatting to the selected cells only.

- ✔ All cells showing "Sum of *fieldname*" values, where *fieldname* is the name of a values field (for example, TotalPrice): Excel applies the conditional formatting to all cells showing Sum of *fieldname* values in the PivotTable, regardless of the field's hierarchical level, and includes subtotals and grand totals. If the displays of the subtotals or grand totals are turned on, this option is useful for summarizations that aren't sums (otherwise the subtotals and grand totals will skew any conditional formatting based on the range of values in the field). An example of a useful summarization for this option is "Average of *fieldname*."

✔ All cells showing "Sum of *fieldname*" values for *RowField* and *ColumnField*, where *fieldname* is the name of a values field (for example, TotalPrice), *RowField* is the name of a row field, and *ColumnField* is the name of a column field. Excel applies the conditional formatting to all cells showing Sum of *fieldname* values in the PivotTable for the row and column fields that correspond to the cells you selected for conditional formatting and excludes subtotals. *ColumnField* is excluded from the option if the PivotTable doesn't include any column fields.

In the preceding list, we assume that the values field is summarized using the Sum function (Excel's default). The actual name for the option depends on the summarization function applied to the field. If the values are averaged, for example, the name will be "All cells showing 'Average of *fieldname*'" values.

Remember: If you select either of the last two options in the preceding list, Excel extends the conditional formatting to include the new data after the PivotTable is refreshed.

Remember: Formatting is applied to a PivotTable in the following order: Direct formatting (for example, formatting that you apply from the Font group on the Ribbon's Home tab) appears over PivotTable style formatting and conditional formatting appears over direct formatting.

Changing the number format of a PivotTable field

In creating a PivotTable report, Excel doesn't retain any special number formatting that you may have applied to your original data. If you apply a currency format to your source data, for example, and then use that data in the PivotTable, Excel doesn't retain the currency formatting in the PivotTable report.

To change the number format for a field in the PivotTable report:

1. Select any cell in the field in which you want to change the number format. Most often, you will use this option to change the number format in the values area of the PivotTable, but you can change the number formats of numeric or date fields in the row or column areas.

2. Right-click and choose Field Settings or Value Field Settings from the contextual menu (the name on the contextual menu depends on whether you're changing the number format of a row or column field or a values field). Excel displays the Field Settings or Value Field Settings dialog box.

3. Click the Number Format button. Excel displays the Format Cells dialog box.

4. In the Category list box, select a number format category and then select a format on the right side of the Format Cells dialog box.

5. Click OK to exit the Format Cells dialog box, and then click OK again to exit the Field Settings or Value Field Settings dialog box.

A quick way to change the number format of cells in a values field is to right-click a cell in the field and then choose Number Format to display the Format Cells dialog box.

Remember: After you apply a number format option using Field Settings, Value Field Settings, or Number Format options in the contextual menu, the formatting is applied to any new data that appears after you refresh the PivotTable. If you want to apply formatting (number, font, background, and so on) to only a cell or a group of cells, select the cell or range, right-click in the selection, choose Format Cells from the contextual menu, and then make your selections in the Format Cells dialog box that appears.

Grouping PivotTable Items

A handy feature enables you to group specific items in a single field of a PivotTable report. If one of the fields in your source data consists of dates, for example, the PivotTable displays a separate row or column for every date. You may find that grouping the dates into months, quarters, or years is a more useful way to create a PivotTable report with a date field.

Remember: If you're grouping by date or number, the field you select for grouping can't have blank items. Also, if you're grouping by date, all cells in the source data date field must carry one of Excel's recognized date or time formats.

Creating a date group

To create a date group PivotTable, follow these steps:

1. Right-click a cell in the date field that you want to group and choose Group from the contextual menu. Excel displays the Grouping dialog box (see Figure 12-6).

2. Select the grouping(s) you want. Note the following when selecting your grouping(s):

   • To select more than one grouping, click each grouping option in turn. Click a grouping option a second time to deselect it.

   • To group weekly or biweekly, select the Days option and specify 7 or 14, respectively, in the Number of Days box.

- If you select a multiple days grouping and then select another grouping (for example, months, quarters, or years), Excel ignores the multiple days group because it's not possible to group across grouping boundaries. For example, if you attempt to group by week and by month, the weekdays can span across two months, so it's impossible to accommodate both groupings simultaneously.

- In the dialog box, Excel automatically chooses the starting and ending dates for the group based on the range of dates in the PivotTable.

3. To manually specify the starting date or ending date or both, clear the check box next to Starting At or Ending At and enter a new date in the text box. For example, if you're grouping by week and want to ensure that the week is grouped from Sunday to Saturday, in the Starting At text box, enter the Sunday date prior to Excel's selected starting date (unless Excel's starting date is Sunday).

4. Click OK. Excel creates the grouping(s).

Figure 12-6

 If your date field covers multiple years and you elect to group by month or quarter or both, you should also include the Years grouping. If you don't include the Years grouping, each month or quarter will be summarized for all years, not for each year.

Creating a number group

If you include a numeric field (or a text field that looks like a number) in the row or column areas of the PivotTable, you can create a number group. For example, if you have a row field with a lot of order or invoice numbers, you might want to create a more compact report. To create a number group, follow these steps:

1. Right-click a cell in the field in which you want to create a number group and choose Group from the menu. Excel displays the Grouping dialog box and automatically chooses the starting and ending numbers for the group.

2. To manually specify the starting number or ending number or both, clear the check box next to Starting At or Ending At and enter a new number in the text box.

3. In the By text box, specify the number that you want to group by.

4. Click OK. Excel creates the grouping.

Creating a text group

Excel allows you to create text groups. A text group might be useful, for example, if you want to group multiple states into sales territories. Follow these steps to create a text group:

1. Select the cells in the field that you want to group. If the items that you want to group aren't next to each other, you can make a multiple selection by holding Ctrl and then selecting the items that will make up the group.

2. Right-click any cell in the selection and choose Group from the contextual menu. Excel automatically creates the group with a generic title, such as Group1, Group2 and so on.

3. To change the name of the group to something more meaningful, click the cell with the new group name and then type a new name in the formula bar.

Modifying a PivotTable Report

A PivotTable is a special type of range, and (except for formatting) you can't manipulate it like a normal range. For example, you can't insert or delete rows, edit results, or move cells. If you attempt to do so, Excel displays an error message. However, you can make certain modifications to the layout or structure of your PivotTable, some of which are described in this section.

Modifying a report layout

When you create a PivotTable, by default Excel uses the new Compact layout, in which the row and column field headings are hidden. This layout is useful if you have many fields in your report because it minimizes horizontal space on the worksheet and can make reading the report easier. You can, however, use one of the following alternative layouts:

- ✔ Outline: This layout is similar to the Compact layout, except it displays the individual field headings.

- ✔ Tabular: In this layout, the first item in a sublevel field appears not on a separate row (refer to Figure 12-1) but on the same row as its upper level (parent) field item.

To change the report layout, click anywhere in the PivotTable, click the Report Layout button on the Design tab, and then choose a layout option from the menu.

With all standard PivotTable layouts, by default, the parent field item names are not repeated when the parent has multiple children. In Figure 12-1, because the subcategory items Bottles and Cages, Helmets, and Tires and Tubes have children in the ProductName field, the cells between each subcategory item are empty (for example, empty cells are between Bottles and Cages and Cleaners, Helmets and Hydration Packs, and so on). The implication of these empty cells is that you can't use lookup and other formulas that work with a traditional table of data.

In Excel 2010, you can fill the empty rows in the PivotTable by repeating the parent item names. Click anywhere in the PivotTable, click the PivotTable Tools Design tab, click the Report Layouts button, and then choose Repeat All Item Labels from the menu.

Remember: The Repeat All Item Labels option applies to *all* fields in the PivotTable. Also, it is best to use the option with the Tabular report layout and any subtotals turned off.

Modifying a report structure

The power behind a PivotTable lies in its ability to display your summarized data in many dimensions by rearranging fields in the row, column, and values areas of the report and adding report filters in the report filter area. Use the following techniques to rearrange the report structure to display your data differently:

- ✔ To add fields to the report, drag the field labels from the field list in the task pane to the appropriate label boxes below the field list. To remove a field from the report, either drag the field label off the appropriate label box or clear the check box next to the field name in the field list.

- ✔ To move fields between the row, column, and report filter areas of the report, drag the field labels between label boxes in the task pane.

- ✔ To rearrange levels in the row or column areas of the report, click and drag a field label in the row or column label box above or below the appropriate field labels in the same label box.

You can move fields also by clicking the field labels in the task pane label boxes and selecting a move option from the menu.

If you have a large PivotTable, you can experience delays after adding, removing, or moving fields in the table because the updates may take some time for Excel to complete. If you're adding, removing, or moving many fields at a time, you can experience multiple delays, which can be annoying. To circumvent the problem, select the Defer Layout Update check box at the bottom of the task pane. Then to update the PivotTable after you complete the structural changes, click the Update button to the right of the Defer Layout Update check box.

Displaying and hiding subtotals and grand totals

Sometimes, you may want to view your report with subtotals above or below a group or you may want to hide the subtotals display. Also, you may want to display grand totals in rows or columns only, or not at all. To change the display option for subtotals, click anywhere in the PivotTable, click the Subtotals button on the Design tab, and then choose an option from the menu. To change the display option for grand totals, click anywhere in the PivotTable, click the Grand Totals button on the Design tab, and then choose an option from the menu.

To turn off subtotals for only a single field, make sure that subtotals are turned on for the entire report, right-click an item in the field, and choose Subtotal *fieldname* from the contextual menu, where *fieldname* is the name of the field whose subtotal you're turning off (for example, ProductName). To display subtotals for only one field, make sure that subtotals are turned off for the entire report, right-click an item in the field, and choose Subtotal *fieldname* from the contextual menu.

Expanding and collapsing field item levels

Expanding field item levels in your PivotTable report allows you to see sublevel item details in your report summary, and collapsing item levels allows you to hide sublevel details in your report summary. Each higher-level field item has a +/– button that expands or collapses all sublevels below the field item. Or expand or collapse to other levels of details as follows:

- ✔ To expand all sublevel items in a field, right-click an item in the field, choose Expand/Collapse from the contextual menu, and then choose Expand Entire Field from the flyout menu. To collapse all sublevel items in a field, repeat the preceding but choose Collapse Entire Field from the flyout menu (see Figure 12-7).

- ✔ To expand a field item down to a specific sublevel, right-click an item in the field, choose Expand/Collapse from the contextual menu, and then choose the field name from the bottom portion of the flyout menu.

Figure 12-7

📋	Copy
📑	Format Cells...
📄	Refresh
	Sort ▸
	Filter ▸
✓	Subtotal "Product Category"
	Expand/Collapse ▸
⇒	Group...
⇐	Ungroup...
	Move ▸
✕	Remove "Product Category"
⊞	Field Settings...
	PivotTable Options...
🔲	Hide Field List

Expand/Collapse flyout menu:

- ⊞ Expand
- ⊟ Collapse
- ⊞ Expand Entire Field
- ⊟ Collapse Entire Field
- Collapse to "Product Category"
- Expand to "Product Subcategory"
- Expand to "ProductName"

Refreshing a PivotTable Report

If the source data that a PivotTable report uses changes, the PivotTable doesn't update automatically. You must refresh the PivotTable manually. To refresh a PivotTable, click a cell in the PivotTable and then click Refresh on the Design tab, or right-click anywhere in the PivotTable and choose Refresh from the contextual menu.

Renaming a PivotTable

After you create a PivotTable, Excel provides a generic name for it, such as PivotTable1, PivotTable2, and so on. It's a good idea to provide a meaningful name for the PivotTable, especially if your workbook has multiple PivotTables. Renaming a PivotTable is simple. Click anywhere in the PivotTable and then click the PivotTable Tools Options tab. On the far left of the Options tab is the PivotTable group. Enter a name in the PivotTable Name box.

Using Custom Calculations

Custom calculations are simply a list of predefined calculations, such as running totals or ratios, that Excel provides to allow you to perform powerful data analysis. Follow these steps to add a custom calculation to a PivotTable:

1. Add the field for which you want to create the custom calculation to the values area of the PivotTable. To see a standard summarization and a custom calculation for the same field, add the field to the values area twice.

2. Click anywhere in the appropriate value field and choose a custom calculation using either of the following methods:

   - Click the PivotTable Tools Options tab on the Ribbon, click the Show Value As button, and then choose an option from the list.

   - Right-click in the value field, choose Show Value As from the menu, and then choose an option from the flyout menu.

3. If necessary, select a base field or a base field and a base item. (Although some custom calculations require no additional user input after you make a selection, others require you to select a base field or a base field and a base item.)

   In Figure 12-8, I added the SalesAmount field several times to the PivotTable to illustrate how you use custom calculations requiring a base

field and a base item. I renamed each added field by clicking the title and
entering a new name in the formula bar.

Figure 12-8

Years	OrderDate	Product Category	Sum of SalesAmount	Month Running Total	Year Running Total	% Diff. from Prev. Month
2007	Jul	Bikes	$473,388.16	$473,388.16	$473,388.16	
	Aug	Bikes	$506,191.69	$979,579.85	$506,191.69	6.93%
	Sep	Bikes	$473,943.03	$1,453,522.89	$473,943.03	-6.37%
	Oct	Bikes	$513,329.47	$1,966,852.36	$513,329.47	8.31%
	Nov	Bikes	$543,993.41	$2,510,845.77	$543,993.41	5.97%
	Dec	Bikes	$755,527.89	$3,266,373.66	$755,527.89	38.89%
2007 Total			**$3,266,373.66**		**$3,266,373.66**	
2008	Jan	Bikes	$596,746.56	$596,746.56	$596,746.56	
	Feb	Bikes	$550,816.69	$1,147,563.25	$550,816.69	-7.70%
	Mar	Bikes	$644,135.20	$1,791,698.45	$644,135.20	16.94%
	Apr	Bikes	$663,692.29	$2,455,390.74	$663,692.29	3.04%
	May	Bikes	$673,556.20	$3,128,946.94	$673,556.20	1.49%
	Jun	Bikes	$676,763.65	$3,805,710.59	$676,763.65	0.48%
	Jul	Bikes	$500,365.16	$4,306,075.74	$973,753.32	-26.07%
	Aug	Bikes	$546,001.47	$4,852,077.21	$1,052,193.16	9.12%
	Sep	Bikes	$350,466.99	$5,202,544.20	$824,410.02	-35.81%
	Oct	Bikes	$415,390.23	$5,617,934.44	$928,719.71	18.52%
	Nov	Bikes	$335,095.09	$5,953,029.53	$879,088.49	-19.33%
	Dec	Bikes	$577,314.00	$6,530,343.53	$1,332,841.89	72.28%
2008 Total			**$6,530,343.53**		**$9,796,717.18**	
2009	Jan	Bikes	$438,865.17	$438,865.17	$1,035,611.73	
	Feb	Bikes	$489,090.34	$927,955.51	$1,039,907.03	11.44%
	Mar	Bikes	$485,574.79	$1,413,530.30	$1,129,709.99	-0.72%
	Apr	Bikes	$506,399.27	$1,919,929.57	$1,170,091.55	4.29%
	May	Bikes	$562,772.56	$2,482,702.13	$1,236,328.76	11.13%
	Jun	Bikes	$554,799.23	$3,037,501.36	$1,231,562.88	-1.42%
	Jul	Bikes	$865,692.78	$3,903,194.14	$1,839,446.10	56.04%
	Aug	Bikes	$772,021.51	$4,675,215.65	$1,824,214.67	-10.82%
	Sep	Bikes	$931,963.95	$5,607,179.60	$1,756,373.97	20.72%
	Oct	Bikes	$999,928.88	$6,607,108.48	$1,928,648.59	7.29%
	Nov	Bikes	$1,116,620.90	$7,723,729.38	$1,995,709.39	11.67%
	Dec	Bikes	$1,635,373.24	$9,359,102.62	$2,968,215.13	46.46%
2009 Total			**$9,359,102.62**		**$19,155,819.80**	
2010	Jan	Bikes	$1,254,568.27	$1,254,568.27	$2,290,180.00	
	Feb	Bikes	$1,377,419.13	$2,631,987.40	$2,417,326.16	9.79%

Figure 12-8 shows a standard summarization and two running totals: one
for Month as the base field and another for Year as the base field. Note
that Excel restarts the running total for each new parent item; you cannot
alter this behavior. For example, Year is the parent of Month, and the
month running totals restart for each year.

If you want to create a month running total that does not reset at the
beginning of each year, you need a field that combines year and month in
a single field. This field must be created in the PivotTable's data source.

Figure 12-8 also shows a percent difference custom calculation. The base
field for the calculation is Month and the base item is Previous (in this
case, the previous month). You can also select a specific item. (For example,
if you select Jan as the base item, Excel will calculate the difference
between the January total and the individual totals for each succeeding
month.)

Remember: All custom calculations are based on the standard sum aggregate for
a value field.

Sorting and Filtering Your Data

In the process of data analysis, you will often want to sort and filter your data. Whether working in tables or PivotTables, Excel provides powerful tools for sorting and filtering your data.

In this part . . .

- ✔ **Creating a Custom Sort List**
- ✔ **Filtering Data in a PivotTable and Table**
- ✔ **Sorting Data in a PivotTable and Table**

Creating a Custom Sort List

Most of your sorting activities will involve sorting a column or field in ascending or descending order. However, sometimes the standard sort options for text fields are not appropriate, such as when sorting days of the weeks or months of the year. A standard alphabetical sort on months will place April and August at the top of an ascending sort and September and October at the top of a descending sort. You usually want the months to appear in the chronological or reverse date order.

Excel includes four custom lists, and you can also define your own. Excel custom lists are as follows:

- **Abbreviated days:** Sun, Mon, Tue, Wed, Thu, Fri, Sat
- **Days:** Sunday, Monday, Tuesday, Wednesday, Thursday, Friday, Saturday
- **Abbreviated months:** Jan, Feb, Mar, Apr, May, Jun, Jul, Aug, Sep, Oct, Nov, Dec
- **Months:** January, February, March, April, May, June, July, August, September, October, November, December

To create a custom list, follow these steps:

1. Click the Ribbon's File tab and then click the Options button. Excel displays the Excel Options dialog box.

2. Click the Advanced tab and scroll down to the General section.

3. At the bottom of the General section, click the Edit Custom Lists button. Excel displays the Custom Lists dialog box. See Figure 13-1.

Figure 13-1

4. In the Custom Lists window, select the New List entry.

5. Enter your list in the List Entries text box. Press Enter after you type each list entry, or separate each entry with a comma.

6. Click Add and then click OK twice to exit the dialog boxes.

Your custom sort list is now available for use in a table, a PivotTable, or even a standard worksheet range.

TIP If you have a range in your worksheet that you want to use as a custom sort list, in Step 4 click in the Import List from Cells box, select the range in the worksheet, and then click the Import button.

Filtering a PivotTable Report

In most ways, filtering a PivotTable is similar to filtering a table (see "Filtering Data in a Table," later in this part). In the case of PivotTables, however, you're filtering summarized data as opposed to a detailed dataset.

Filtering a PivotTable based on individual field items

Follow these steps to filter fields in your PivotTable based on individual field items:

1. Click the arrow on the header of the row or column field that you want to filter. If you're using the Compact report layout, the individual field headings aren't shown but are represented by a Row Labels header (in the row area), a Column Labels header (in the column area), or both. Click the arrow on the Row Labels or Column Labels header. Excel displays sort and filter options. Figure 13-2 shows the sort and filter options in the Compact Report Layout.

2. If you're using the Compact report layout, you must first choose the field you want to filter in the Select Field drop-down list. The lower portion of the window displays the field items in a window. By default, Excel selects all items. If you want to display one or only a few entries, you can clear the Select All check box and select the items you want displayed. Alternatively, if you want to *hide* only a few items, clear the check boxes next to these items but do not clear the Select All check box.

3. Click OK. In the PivotTable, Excel displays the items you selected in Step 2 and hides all cleared items. Excel also adds a filter icon (a small funnel) to the field drop-down arrow and to the right of the field label in the task pane to indicate that a filter is applied to the field.

Figure 13-2

4. To filter additional fields, repeat Steps 2 and 3.

 If your PivotTable includes a report filter, you can select multiple items to display or filter by clicking the report filter drop-down arrow and then selecting or deselecting items in the window. Make sure that the Select Multiple Items check box is selected.

Filtering a PivotTable based on a field text search

The procedures for filtering a PivotTable based on a field text search are similar to the procedures outlined for filtering a table based on a column text search. *See* "Filtering a table based on a column text search," later in this part.

If you're using the Compact report layout, you must first choose the field you want to filter from the Select Field drop-down list in the Row Labels or Column Labels sort and filter options (click the arrow next to Row Labels or Column Labels to display the options). *See* "Filtering a PivotTable based on individual field items," immediately preceding this section.

Filtering a PivotTable based on field data type

Similar to tables, a field can be filtered by data type (that is, value, label, or date).

To filter a PivotTable field based on date, number, or label criteria, follow these steps:

1. Click the arrow on the field header of the field you want to filter. If you're using the Compact report layout, individual field headings aren't shown. In this case, click the arrow on Row Labels or Column Labels. Excel displays the sort and filter options.

2. If you're using the Compact report layout, you must first choose the field you want to filter from the Select Field drop-down list. Above the field items window, choose the *datatype* Filters option (where *datatype* is Label, Number, or Date, depending on the data type of the field you're filtering). Each row or column field in a PivotTable has either a Value filter and a Label filter or a Value filter and a Date filter.

3. Choose a filter option from the flyout menu.

4. Complete the dialog box for the filter option and then click OK.

Clearing PivotTable filters

During your analysis of the data in a PivotTable, you may have applied multiple filters to one or more fields. You can manually remove the filters one by one, but Excel provides a quicker way to remove filters from your PivotTable:

✔ To clear filters from a single field, click the arrow on the field header of the field from which you want to remove filters (either on the PivotTable or the task pane field list). If you're using the Compact report layout, click the arrow on Row Labels or Column Labels to display the sort and filter options. Then choose Clear Filter from *fieldname*, where *fieldname* is the name of the field whose filters you're clearing (for example, ProductName). If you're using the Compact report layout, you must first choose the field from which you want to remove the filters from the Select Field drop-down list from the sort and filter options.

✔ To clear all filters in the PivotTable, click anywhere in the PivotTable, click the Sort & Filter button on the Ribbon's Home tab, and then choose Clear from the menu.

Filtering Data in a Table

Filtering data is one of the most common activities performed with a table. Often, you want to view or analyze a subset of the data in a large dataset. When Excel creates a table, it includes a sort-and-filter drop-down arrow to the right of each column header. After you filter your table, the status bar displays the number of rows visible.

Remember: You can use Excel's filtering features in a standard (non-table) range. Select the range, click the Sort & Filter button on the Ribbon's Home tab, and choose Filter from the menu to add the Sort & Filter drop-down arrows to the header row. A worksheet can have only one sort and filter range but can have many tables, each with its own sort and filter settings.

Remember: If your table data was imported from an external range, your table filters and sort orders are normally reapplied after you refresh the range (import the latest data). If you add data rows manually, however, you must click the Sort & Filter button on the Ribbon's Home tab and then choose Reapply from the menu before Excel will update the table.

Filtering a table based on individual column entries

Follow these steps to filter your table data based on the individual entries in a column:

1. Click the arrow on the header of the column you want to filter. Excel displays the sort and filter options (see Figure 13-3).

Figure 13-3

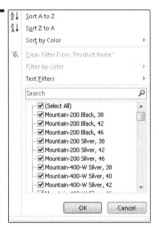

2. The lower portion of the window displays the *unique* column entries in a window. By default, Excel selects all entries. If you want to display rows for one or only a few entries, clear the Select All check box and individually select the items you want displayed. Alternatively, if you want to *hide* rows for only a few entries, clear the check boxes next to these entries but do not clear the Select All check box.

   Note that the list can display a maximum of 10,000 *unique* entries in the column.

3. Click OK. In the table, Excel displays rows for all the entries you selected in Step 2 and hides all rows for the cleared entries. If your table uses an alternative row-banding style, the banding is preserved after you filter table rows. Excel also adds a filter icon (a small funnel) on the column drop-down to indicate that a filter is applied to the column.

4. To filter additional columns, repeat Steps 2 and 3.

If your column has a series of date entries (month, day, year), Excel allows you to filter at the year, month, or day levels. In the column items list window, only the year level is listed initially. If you click the plus sign (+) next to a year, the months for that year are listed. Clicking the plus sign next to the month displays individual day entries for that month.

Filtering a table based on a column text search

Excel 2010 provides a powerful new column filter in the form of a text search box, located just above the individual items list in the column sort and filter drop-down list. This new filter is useful in two significant ways:

- ✔ Because the individual items list in the column sort and filter drop-down list is limited to displaying a maximum of 10,000 unique items, you cannot use this filter if your data set might contain more than the display limit. The search box overcomes this problem.

- ✔ Even if you don't exceed the column filter drop-down list's display limit, it can be tedious scrolling through a large list looking for items to filter.

You can use the search box to include items to filter (remain visible) or to exclude items to filter.

Follow these steps to *include* items in your filter list:

1. Click the column sort and filter arrow. In the search box, enter the first item you want to include in your filter. As you type, Excel filters the list based on the characters you enter (see Figure 13-4).

Figure 13-4

2. As the list narrows, you can select all or some items. To exclude items, clear the check boxes next to the items.

3. After you finish making your selections, select the box labeled Add Current Selection to Filter.

4. Click OK. Excel filters the table to show only the items you selected.

5. If you want to include additional items in your filter list, repeat Steps 1–4.

When you're adding additional items to your filter list, if you don't select the box labeled Add Current Selection to Filter, the new items will *replace* the previous filter list instead of being added to the previous filter list.

Follow these steps to *exclude* items from your filter list:

1. Follow Steps 1 and 2 in the preceding procedure.

2. After you finish making your selections, select the box labeled Add Current Selection to Filter and *deselect* the box labeled (Select All Search Results). These actions effectively exclude items from your filter — that is, everything else is automatically selected.

Remember: The search text you enter is *not* case-sensitive.

You can combine the two techniques discussed in this section into a single filter. Suppose that you've narrowed the list of items you want to include in your filter but you still want to exclude some items. To accomplish this task, follow the steps for the first procedure and then the steps for the second procedure.

You can use *wildcard* characters in your search. Use the * character to represent one or more characters before, between, or after any search text you enter. For example, *500*Black* will locate all items with 500 and Black in the name, with any number of characters before 500, between 500 and Black, and after Black. On the other hand, ?500?Black? will locate all items with only a single character before 500, between 500 and Black, and after Black. You can combine wildcard characters in your search text.

Filtering a table based on column data type

Suppose you have a table column that contains dates. But instead of filtering the column based on individual dates, you want to display dates for the current month, last month, last quarter, or year to date. Or suppose you have a numeric column and want to display records exceeding a certain value or lying between two values. Or perhaps you have a text column and you want to display records that begin with certain text or contain certain text. Excel provides many filtering options that you can apply based on the type of data you have in a column.

To filter table data based on date, number, or text criteria, follow these steps:

1. Click the arrow on the header of the column you want to filter. Excel displays the sort and filter options.

2. Immediately above the window that displays individual column entries, choose the *datatype* Filters option (where *datatype* is Text, Number, or Date, depending on the data type of the column you're filtering).

3. Choose a specific filter option from the flyout menu or choose Custom Filter at the bottom of the menu to display a dialog box that offers additional options.

4. If your choice in Step 3 displays a dialog box, complete the dialog box options and then click OK.

Filtering a table based on cell color

Excel allows you to filter by cell color. Colors are cell background or font colors applied manually or by conditional formatting. Colors can also include color scales and icon sets.

Remember: You can filter by only one color at a time.

To filter your table data based on color formatting, follow these steps:

1. Click the arrow on the header of the column with the color formatting you want to filter. Excel displays the sort and filter options.

2. Choose Filter by Color, and then choose a color option from the flyout menu. You can also choose the No Fill option to filter out all cells with font or background formatting.

Remember: Colors for filtering do *not* include colors defined in the table style, so your table formatting is preserved after color filtering.

Clearing table filters

While analyzing data in a table, you may have applied multiple filters to one or more columns. You can manually remove the filters one by one, but Excel provides a quicker way to remove filters from your table:

✔ To clear filters from a single column, click the arrow on the column header of the column from which you want to remove filters. Then, from the sort and filter options, choose Clear Filter from *columnname*, where *columnname* is the name of the column whose filters you're clearing (for example, ProductName).

✔ To clear all filters in the table, click anywhere in the table, click the Sort & Filter button on the Ribbon's Home tab, and then choose Clear from the menu.

Sorting Data in a PivotTable

Sorting a PivotTable involves rearranging row or column field items so that the items appear in ascending, descending, or a custom order. You may, for example, want to sort a row field of customers or sales regions alphabetically. You can sort numerically, alphabetically, or by date, depending on the data type.

Remember: Unlike a table, Excel sorts items hidden in a filtered field, so that if you remove the filter, the field remains sorted.

The following rules apply when you sort a row or column field:

✔ If you have more than one row or column field in your PivotTable and you sort the outermost row or column field, Excel sorts all the other row or column fields in ascending order, regardless of the sort order you choose for the outermost field.

✔ If you sort the innermost row or column field, Excel does not sort the other row or column fields.

✔ If you sort an intermediate row or column field, Excel sorts fields inner to that field in ascending order, regardless of the sort order you choose for the intermediate field. Excel does not sort fields outer to the intermediate field.

In the context of the PivotTable structure, an *inner* row field is any field to the right of another field. An *outer* field is any field to left of another field. An *inner* column field is any field below another field. An *outer* field is any field above another field.

Sorting a row or column field using standard sort options

Follow these steps to sort a row or column field in your PivotTable using the standard sort options:

1. Click the arrow on the header of the field that you want to sort. If you're using the Compact report layout, individual field headings aren't shown. In this case, click the arrow on Row Labels or Column Labels. Excel displays the sort and filter options.

2. If you're using the Compact report layout, you must first choose the field you want to sort from the Select Field drop-down list from the Row Labels or Column Labels sort and filter options.

3. Choose one of the sort direction options at the top of the window. The options depend on the data type in the column you're sorting (numeric, text, or date). After you choose an option, Excel rearranges the items in the field.

After you apply a sort to a field, Excel adds a small arrow to the field header arrow, indicating the direction of the sort. The arrow also serves as a reminder that you've applied a sort to the field.

Sorting a value field

In some cases, you may want to sort based on the data in the values area of the PivotTable. For instance, you may want to sort sales numbers from largest to smallest.

To sort based on data in the values area, right-click any cell in the value column you want to sort, choose Sort from the contextual menu, and then select a sort direction from the flyout menu. Excel sorts the items in the innermost row field, along with their corresponding values.

You can also sort row-wise instead or column-wise. Right-click any cell in the value row you want to sort, choose Sort from the contextual menu, and then select More Sort options from the flyout menu. In the Sort by Value dialog box, select a sort option (Smallest to Largest or Largest to Smallest) and then select Left to Right for the sort direction. Click OK, and Excel sorts the items in the innermost column field, along with their corresponding values.

Sorting a row or column field manually

When the standard ascending or descending sort order doesn't apply for a field, you can arrange the field items manually. If you have many items you need to arrange manually, it's better to use a custom sort order. *See* "Sorting a row or column field using a custom sort order," immediately following this section.

To rearrange an item manually, click the item to select it. Position the mouse pointer at the edge of the selection until a black arrow cross is displayed at the tip of the pointer. Then hold down the left mouse button and drag the item to its new location.

Sorting a row or column field using a custom sort order

In some cases, you may want to sort a text field in an order other than alphabetical ascending or descending. If your data consists of month names, for example, you probably want them to appear in chronological date order rather than alphabetically. Excel includes four custom lists, and you can also define your own. To sort one or more columns by a custom list, follow these steps:

1. Complete Steps 1–3 in "Sorting a row or column field using standard sort options," except in Step 3, choose More Sort Options instead of one of the sort direction options. Excel displays the Sort dialog box. See Figure 13-5, left.

2. Click More Options. Excel displays the More Sort Options dialog box. See Figure 13-5, right.

Figure 13-5

3. Deselect the Sort Automatically Every Time the Report Is Updated check box.

4. In the First Sort Key Order drop-down list, select an option. Click OK twice to exit the dialog boxes.

Remember: If you need to use a custom list, create it before following the preceding procedure. *See* "Creating a Custom Sort List," earlier in this part.

Sorting Data in a Table

Sorting a table involves rearranging the rows so they're in ascending or descending order, based on the values in one or more columns. You may, for example, want to sort a table of salespeople alphabetically by last name or by sales region. You can sort numerically, alphabetically, or by date, depending on the data.

If you sort a filtered table, Excel sorts only the visible rows. After you remove the filtering from the table, the table is no longer sorted. Therefore, you should remove any column filters before sorting the table.

Remember: You need to re-sort your table after adding (and perhaps editing) table rows. To re-sort the table, click any cell in the table, click the Sort & Filter button on the Design tab, and then choose Reapply from the menu. *See also* "Filtering Data in a Table," earlier in this part.

Sorting a single column based on column values

Follow these steps to sort a single column in your table based on the data in the table:

1. Click the arrow on the header of the column you want to sort. Excel displays the sort and filter options.

2. Choose one of the sort direction options at the top of the window. The options depend on the data type in the column you're sorting (numeric, text, or date). After you choose an option, Excel rearranges the rows in the table.

After you apply a sort to a column, Excel adds a small arrow to the column header arrow, indicating the direction of the sort. The arrow also serves as a reminder that you've applied a sort to the column.

Sorting multiple columns based on column values

Follow these steps to sort multiple columns in your table based on the data in the table:

1. Click the arrow on the header of any column in the table. Excel displays the sort and filter options.

2. Choose Sort by Color and then choose Custom Sort from the flyout menu. Excel displays the Sort dialog box.

3. From the following drop-down lists, choose the options for the first column you want to sort:

   • Column: Choose the first column you want to sort by.

   • Sort On: Choose Values.

   • Order: Choose a sort order.

4. For each additional column you want to sort, click the Add Level button. Each time you do so, new drop-down lists appear. Repeat Step 3 for each sort level you add (see Figure 13-6).

Figure 13-6

Column		Sort On		Order		
Sort by	Month	Values		January, February, March, April,		
Then by	Product Name	Values		A to Z		
Then by	Sales Amount	Cell Color				On Top

5. If you want your sorts to be case-sensitive (applicable to text columns only), click the Options button and then select the Case Sensitive check box. When you make your sorts case-sensitive, uppercase letters appear before lowercase letters in an ascending sort. Normally, sorting ignores the case of letters.

6. If you want to change the sort order of a column after you add several sort levels, click the left side of the sort level and then click the up or down arrow button. If you want to delete a sort level, click the left side of the sort level and then click the Delete Level button. After you click a sort level, Excel highlights the level so you know which level you're deleting or reordering.

7. Click OK, and Excel rearranges the table's rows.

Note that you can sort on up to 64 columns.

Sorting based on a custom sort order

In some cases, you may want to sort a text column in an order other than alphabetical ascending or descending. If your data consists of month names, for example, you probably want them to appear in month order rather than alphabetically. Excel includes four custom lists, and you can also define your own. To sort one or more columns by a custom list, follow these steps:

1. Complete Steps 1–3 in "Sorting multiple columns based on column values," except in Step 3, choose Custom List from the Order drop-down list. Excel displays the Custom Lists dialog box.

2. In the Custom Lists list box, choose a sort order list.

3. Click OK to add the custom list to the Order drop-down list in the Sort dialog box.

4. Click OK. Excel rearranges the table's rows based on the custom order.

You can also create a custom list in the Custom Lists list box. To create a custom list, follow these steps:

1. In the Custom Lists list box, select the NEW LIST entry.

2. In the List Entries text box, type your entries in the order you want your list sorted. Press Enter after you type each entry of the list, or separate each entry with a comma.

3. Click Add to include your new list in the Custom Lists list box.

4. Click your new list and then click OK to add your list to the Order drop-down list in the Sort dialog box.

5. Click OK. Excel rearranges the table's rows based on your custom order.

See also "Creating a Custom Sort List," earlier in this part.

Sorting based on color or conditional formatting icons

You can sort by background or font colors applied to cells manually or by conditional formatting. You can also sort by conditional formatting icon sets or color scales. Sorting by color is useful if you want to group data that meets a conditional formatting criterion.

Follow these steps to sort columns based on color (or icon):

1. Click the arrow on the header of the column that you want to sort by color (or icon). Excel displays the sort and filter options.

2. If you want to sort by a single color, choose Sort by Color and choose a color (or icon, if applicable) from the flyout menu. After you choose a color option, Excel moves the rows with that color to the top of the table.

 A quick way to sort by a single color is to right-click a cell in the column with the color, choose Sort from the contextual menu, and then choose an appropriate color sort option (cell color, cell font, or cell icon).

You can sort by more than one color if, for example, you have multiple colors in a column based on conditional formatting conditions or you want to arrange color scale colors or icon set icons in a particular order in a column. *See also* "Formatting a Range Using Comparative Visualizations," in Part 8, for a discussion of color scales and icon sets. Follow these steps to sort by more than one color in a column:

1. Complete the preceding steps to sort by the first color.

2. Click the arrow on the column header, choose Sort by Color, and then choose Custom Sort from the flyout menu. Excel displays the Sort dialog box with the first sort level listed (refer to Figure 13-6).

3. Click the left side of the existing sort level and then click the Copy Level button. Excel adds a new sort level with identical sort conditions.

4. Click the Order drop-down list and choose a color (or icon if applicable) for the new sort level.

5. Repeat Steps 3 and 4 to add additional sort levels, except in Step 3, click the left side of the last sort level added before clicking Copy Level.

6. Click OK. Excel rearranges the table's rows in the color order you specified.

Index

Notes